ATTITUDE 13

A Daughter of Guam's Collection of Short Stories

Hafa Adai, Jenny! Enjoy!

[signature] 2010

Tanya Chargualaf Taimanglo

authorHOUSE®

AuthorHouse™
1663 Liberty Drive
Bloomington, IN 47403
www.authorhouse.com
Phone: 1-800-839-8640

©2010 Tanya Chargualaf Taimanglo. All rights reserved.

No part of this book may be reproduced, stored in a retrieval system, or transmitted by any means without the written permission of the author.

First published by AuthorHouse 9/9/2010

ISBN: 978-1-4520-7242-5 (e)
ISBN: 978-1-4520-7241-8 (sc)
ISBN: 978-1-4520-7240-1 (hc)

Library of Congress Control Number: 2010912753

Printed in the United States of America

This book is printed on acid-free paper.

Because of the dynamic nature of the Internet, any Web addresses or links contained in this book may have changed since publication and may no longer be valid. The views expressed in this work are solely those of the author and do not necessarily reflect the views of the publisher, and the publisher hereby disclaims any responsibility for them.

For Henry, Elijah and Samantha--my sun, moon and stars.

Si Yu'os Ma'ase to dad (R.I.P.), omma, Sonny, Alison Taimanglo Cuasay, Lee Cuasay, Auntie Patty Taimanglo, Kimberly Untalan Taisipic and especially, *Siñora Dolores Aguon--who carries on my father's work.*

Contents

Resurfacing	1
By Any Other Name	9
Sand	19
Flightless Bird	25
Goddess	33
Yes, I Am.	45
Apostle's Creep	59
Chirika's Pepper Plant*	67
The List	77
Skin Tag You're It	81
The Tigress Club	85
Echoes	89
Off Road	97
Chamorro Word/Phrase KEY	103

RESURFACING

I drew the warm air into my mouth, and it left a cool trail to my lungs. It wasn't painful to breathe again, but I sat on the moist sand and thought about each breath for some time. How long had I been in the ocean?

My wish had been granted, to be among those who walk the land. I thought I returned to the spot I walked out on my former life, but the shores of my home looked so different. I wanted to run to my home by the river, but my legs felt heavy. It was like I was in a dream. I clawed at the sand; it was dawn on Guam. I didn't realize that my hair had grown so long, like black seaweed that nearly reached my feet. Remnants of my former shape were still visible on my legs.

There was an occasional roar behind me and I was not frightened. I had encountered very scary creatures in the ocean, amongst all the beauty. I just wanted to see my mother and godmother one more time.

I realized my nakedness and I looked around for some form of cover.

That's when I saw towering white cliffs in the dim morning light. These weren't like any cliffs I had ever scene. Bright lights shone through a line of holes. The lines on these cliffs were straight. Some of the structures were higher than the others and I saw movement in them. Were these caves?

I then heard footsteps coming towards me, quick and rhythmic. I pulled my hair forward and it served as a blanket over my body. The last of the shiny scales disappeared from my legs. I did not move. I did not want whoever was approaching to see me. I kept my eyes on the sparkling ebony water and wondered if I had made a mistake in wishing to come home. King, my ocean father, said I could always return if I submerged myself in the water and swim back to the trench. He warned that it would be the last time he would grant me the wish to return to the shore. The change would be permanent.

The clomping feet slowed and I heard heavy breathing. A crackling sound made me shift towards the person and I heard the woman's fear in her high-pitched squeal.

"Oh my God!" There was a clattering of sounds as she dropped her brown bag of things. "Miss? Are you okay?"

I did not understand her words as I pushed my damp hair off my face. It didn't sound like the language I knew. Something in me told me she was friendly. I tried to speak, but my words could not escape. I cleared my throat and then the flood of sounds exploded forth. It was a cluster of odd notes and from the look on the pretty woman's face, I could tell she was frightened. She stumbled back and I decided not to move. She had her hands over her ears and a pained look on her face.

"I can't understand. Is your throat hurt? Damn, you can shatter glass with that voice."

I cleared my throat again, rubbing my hands on my neck. The slits on the side of my neck were nearly smoothed out. I tried again. "*Guahu si Raina.*"

"Oh, I don't speak Chamorro. Well, I took it in high school, but I don't remember much. *Siñot* Benavente would kill me." The woman spoke quickly in her language. She smiled and I was thankful for her kindness. "*Guahu*, hmm. You are Raina?"

"*Hunggan! Guahu si Raina!*" I said.

"*Guahu si Maia.*"

"Maia. *Hafa tatamanu hao?*"

"*Todu maolek.*" Maia jumped up and down. "Awesome. I totally remember that!"

"*Taotao Hagåtña yo'.*"

"You are from Agana, I mean *Hagåtña*? This is Tumon." Maia pointed to the ground. "Where's your house? I mean, these are all hotels here."

"Hoh-tels. *Este*, hotels?"

"Raina, you are totally naked. Here." Maia gave me her white garment, too short to be a dress. It barely covered my bottom. Maia turned away so I could dress. I slid my arms into the clothing and waited. Maia turned around and gasped.

"Oh, Raina, you need to zip the hoodie up, then no one will see your *susu*."

"*Susu!*" I smiled and placed my hands on my chest. She said another word I understood.

"You are too funny, and wow. You are incredibly beautiful. *Bunita*. Maybe I should call the police." Maia pulled on a shiny sliver and it enveloped me in the soft white clothing, covering my chest. "You only speak Chamorro, huh? Are you from Rota or Saipan?"

I didn't understand her once again. A man ran past us and Maia stood in front of me protectively. I smiled at him and he began running backwards. He smiled back at me and nearly stumbled.

"Keep moving, pervert!" Maia yelled at him. She pushed my long hair behind my shoulders and smiled. "What are we going to do with you? *Guma*? Where, um, *mangge guma* or is it, *manu guma?*"

I smiled and looked around. The rising sun revealed my surroundings. I didn't recognize anything. I pointed to the ground again and said, "*Tomhom?*"

"Yes. This is *Tomhom*."

I looked to the water and recognized the cliff I used to swim to as a child. I wondered how long I was with King in the ocean. I was nearly as tall as Maia. She looked old enough to be with a man, and old enough to be a mother. I must be that old too, if not older.

I walked towards the cliff I recognized. My home should be close, but I wasn't very sure. There were so many white cliffs, hotels, that I wondered if mama would still be living in our house. Maia followed behind me and offered a strange, red item from her bag. It was filled with liquid which looked like blood. She opened the top and let me smell the juice. It smelled sweet, but I didn't want to drink blood. Maia drank and placed the object under my nose again. "Try it. Drink. Um, *chagi*? Ga-tor-ade."

I grasped the object and smelled it again. I stuck my tongue into the hole and let the taste settle in my mouth. It was delicious. Sweet. It was like mango or papaya, but nothing I've ever tried. I tilted the object and let all the sweet juice empty into my mouth. I didn't realize I was so hungry. I returned the empty container to Maia. I drank all the juice and I felt ashamed. "*Dispensa yo'*."

"It's okay. You must be hungry. I'll follow you to your *guma*, then I'll be on my way. I have classes later." Maia smiled. "I don't know why

I even bother, you can't understand English. Are you sure you're not from like Tinian or somewhere?"

I followed closely behind Maia. The ground switched from sand to rock to a black sheet of hardness. My feet had not been used in so long my grunts of pain did not go unnoticed by Maia. We reached a large shiny box. It was red too. The round black objects holding the red box up were as tall as my waist.

"This is my Jeep. I think I have an extra pair of *zori* for you." Maia opened a door and pointed to a chair. "Get in. Um, *siya*."

I pulled myself up. It was like climbing a tree. Maia giggled as I'm sure my *dagan* was in her view. "Wait!" She ran to the back of this Jeep. "Here. Put these shorts on and these *zoris*." She grabbed my legs and placed it in the garment, pulling it up and dressing me like I was a child. She then helped me into the Jeep.

The glorious sunshine unveiled the rest of the island. I did not recognize anything except for coconut trees and latte stones, which must have shrunk since I was last here. I wondered if this was even Guam. Did King bring me to the correct shore?

Maia hopped into the chair next to me and smiled. She placed a tiny object into a hole and twisted it. The loud roar of this thing she called a Jeep startled me. I grasped the chair and stuck my head out of the window.

"No! Raina. I'm sorry. It's just the Jeep. It's a loud one. Please, sit down." The ground was so far from my perch, I did what I was told. Raina grabbed a stick by a large black circle and pulled it. The Jeep moved backwards and I held onto the door. This time I stifled my scream. As the Jeep moved forward the breeze helped me relax. Raina pointed to a group of silver and black circles. "Music?"

I shrugged my shoulders and pointed to the circles too. "Mu-zic."

Maia pushed a black circle and a loud blaring and pounding started.

"Oh, crap! Sorry." With a twist of her wrist, the pounding lowered in volume and a beautiful female voice began singing in the language Maia spoke.

We continued on a path and the trees and hotels blurred from the speed. When we stopped, I saw other colorful boxes of different sizes around me. People, different types of people looked up at me. I smiled and they smiled in return. Why was Guam so different? It looked different and smelled different. Maia didn't even speak Chamorro. My chest tightened as I thought of the possibility of my mama being dead. Would my nina be gone too?

"We're in *Hagåtña* now. Where do I go? I don't know of any homes around here. Maybe you meant *Hagåtña* Heights?"

I saw the shoreline and smelled the rich ocean air. Nothing was familiar. The green I was used to was replaced by squares and large structures that looked like the hotels. Then something caught my eye. It was a fish girl like me.

"Maia!" I pointed to a green clearing and a bridge.

"What? Do you see your house?" I placed my arm on Maia's shoulder and pointed to the fish girl I saw. Within a few moments, Maia rotated her Jeep and stopped. I started to climb out the small window, but Maia pulled me back, reached over me and then the door swung open.

I jumped out and began running, the hot ground was hard under my feet, but it didn't hurt with the *zori* on. I stumbled a few times and then I saw her. She was frozen. Unmoving. A fish girl not in the water. I reached out slowly and touched her tail. Hard and warm. Was she real? Was she made of stone? Did someone turn her into stone? Her skin was one color, as dark as the night. Her hair covered one *susu* and she was looking to the sky. Her fish tail was covered in scales larger than I had.

"Listen, Raina. Don't go off running like that." Maia was breathing hard.

"*Hayi?*" I pointed to the fish girl.

"That's *Sirena*. She's our mermaid legend. You know girl and fish? *Palao'an yan guihan?*" I looked at her again. The fine features of her stone face did not look like mine. Why didn't she move? I walked around her. I pushed on her hard back. Nothing. Maia began to giggle. "What ever are you doing, Raina? *Hafa?*"

I shook my head and said, "*Palao'an yan guihan.*" This was not the home I wanted to return to. Nobody here was like me. Nothing made sense. I looked across a path of gray with traveling shiny boxes and saw the ocean. I tugged on the little shiny tab on the white garment Maia let me wear. I handed the clothing to Maia. I looked at the statue again and pulled my hair over my chest to cover my *susu*. I wiggled out of the other clothing and kicked off the *zoris*.

"What are you doing, Raina? You're going to cause an accident!" I began to walk to the water, the only thing I knew now. I looked back to Maia and waved. She stood with her mouth open, but did not move. My feet padded over a patch of grass, then more hard, gray trails. When I reached the sand, Maia was gone. Her red Jeep was in motion. I stood at the shore's edge and let the warm water lick my toes. I turned around to find a few people watching me now. As I looked at the rising cliffs beyond the motionless fish girl, I saw a landscape I vaguely remembered. This was not my home. I had been gone too long and now everyone I loved must be gone. When I became a creature of the sea, I left at this location and mama and *nina* were on the shore. But, the place my house should have been was overtaken by these hotels.

I saw Maia stop her Jeep and run towards me. "Raina! Where are you going? Wait. My auntie's coming. You can tell her where your home is, she speaks Chamorro. Please." I smiled at Maia, the girl who clothed me and greeted me and was protective. I waved and turned to the ocean. My feet began to tingle and I knew my retransformation was beginning. I walked towards the horizon until the warm water was deep enough. I dove in and swam parallel to the shore. Maia ran and kept up with me. My legs locked together and the bones became soft. My change did not hurt like the first time. I knew what to expect. I ran my fingers along my waist and felt the scales. I emerged from the water to see Maia again, this time she was waist high in the warm ocean water. I wanted her to know what I was and I didn't want her to think I was a girl lost.

I swam up to her quietly and swiftly under water. I peeked my head up from the blue. She was startled still looking out to the spot she watched me submerge. "Raina, I can help you. Please." She held her hand out to me. I took it.

"*Si Yu'os Ma'ase*, Maia. *Guahu si Raina. Guahu Palao'an yan guihan.*" I released her hand and swam away from her. I dove and waved my fins above water. My revelation had the effect I wanted. Maia had the same surprised face my mama had once. She looked around to see if anyone else might be witness to what she was seeing. The few people walking continued on their paths. As the distance increased between us, I plunged into the deep and propelled myself out of the water. The air was cool as I floated to the clouds. I waved my tail one last time and broke my return to the warm water with my hands. I raced to the trench, ready for the second time in my life to be one with the ocean.

BY ANY OTHER NAME

"Grandma's dead, Toni." Roque said over the phone.

Good! I thought. "That's terrible," I said.

"Can you make it home for the funeral? It's in ten days, since dad's waiting for Auntie Checha to fly out from Virginia, Space A." My brother asked like I had a choice in the matter.

It's just like grandma to die during my finals week. I thought. "I'll start checking flights on-line," I said.

My brother's call lit a fuse in me. Anger tried to find space in my head, where stress was the current tenant. I had two final exams tackled and three to go, and now this crap about grandma dying. My dad's mom was the last of the quartet of grandparents to go. My least favorite one, not only because I was bestowed with her antiquated name, but because she was a mean bitch. I have the welt marks on my butt and thighs to prove it. The scars on my forearms, barely visible to others, but permanent with the memories of her thick nails pinching me in church or at her ranch only allowed resentment to fester in my soul. I was the only grandchild of ten to be awarded such treatment.

"Toni!" My pseudo boyfriend called from outside my apartment building.

I took my time reaching the window; the air was still cool even though the Hawaiian sun blazed high in the sky. I traded off a college education on Guam for another island paradise where I could still wear shorts and tanks and *zoris* comfortably. It was also good to be freed from my parent's controlling clutches. The first day I arrived in Hawaii, I treated myself to a tattoo on my right hip. A Yin and Yang meant rebellion lying beneath my clothes.

"Toni! Get down here."

"God, Tyler! Can't you just text me or call like a normal person?"

"Isn't this more romantic? I'm beckoning while your heaving breast hang over your balcony. Toni-punzel, let down your hair! Want me to sing?" It took all my self-control not to hurl my potted sunflower at him.

"Please don't! I'll be down soon." I grabbed my keys and headed for the stairs as a tone deaf Tyler began a serenade.

Tyler was as third generation Japanese-American in Hawaii. His physique caught my attention first. His long surfer boy hair was a surefire way to piss off my dad. Tyler's face was easy to look at, but it was his overall lack of fire that left me wanting more.

My dad let it slip to grandma that I was dating him and I could imagine her *muyo'* and the disapproving click of her tongue. The first thing she asked was if I was "shacking up with the Jap." Grandma was a survivor of the Japanese occupation on Guam and she found it ironic that our island was now being sustained by Japanese tourism. Part of me knew that I continued to date Tyler because it irked my grandma. I wondered what would become of our relationship now that she was dead.

I lead the way to our usual haunt. I shoved my hands in my pockets so Tyler couldn't hold my hand. He settled for inserting his hand in the back pocket of my jean shorts. We settled into the booth we visited a hundred times. Even with the lunch crowd, our order came quick.

I stared into my bowl of ramen as Tyler rattled on about his finals. He was a criminal justice major and I was a history major. For someone who wanted so badly to leave Guam, I don't know why I decided to minor in Pacific Islander Studies. All my research was Guam based. I guess you do what you know.

The steam from the perfect universe of my ramen enveloped me and I realized that I should have been securing a ticket home. I should have been studying too, but my brain was numb as Tyler was quoting his Facebook posts, like I didn't already read them.

"My grandma is dead." I spoke into the bowl. I wanted Tyler to stop talking.

"Whoa. I'm sorry. Don't you hate her? You said so once." He slurped his steaming noodles.

"When did I ever mention her before now?" I looked up at Tyler and stabbed my chopsticks in my soup, ruining its perfection. Tyler squirmed and made a face. He once told me that it was bad luck to stab my food with my chopsticks. I was supposed to rest the chopsticks on the brim of my bowl. If I accepted that cultural practice, then maybe Tyler would think I loved him.

I made it a point to never speak about my family to him because I never intended on becoming Mrs. Tomita. The less he knew about me, the easier it was to break ties.

"Last week. You were way drunk, dude." I hated it when Tyler called me "*brah*" or "dude."

"I don't think so. *You* must have been drunk." I said.

"I quote, 'My grandma is a wicked witch who lives in a cave on Guam. She eats babies and uses their bones for jewelry.' I thought you were explaining another Guam legend to me, *brah*."

I glared at Tyler and realized that I would say something as venomous as that. I also realized that Tyler knew entirely too much about me, the real me. It was time to release him from my little bubble. I slowly untied the raffia bracelet dotted with small red hibiscus beads—a gift on our first and only Valentine's together. I slid it across the cold blue table, along with a wrinkled twenty dollar bill. I couldn't expect Tyler to pay for our last meal.

"It's time."

"Time for what?" Tyler asked. His little boy giggle was not so charming now. "You haven't even touched your noodles, dude. Are we breaking up? Are you serious?"

"Time to end this. Not hungry. Yes and yes." I answered Tyler's questions. My chair screeched like an angry owl as I stood to leave the diner. "You bore me, *brah* and graduation is around the corner. I'm not sure about grad school, dude. I can't even afford it. Anyway, I'm going home to Guam to bury the witch."

Two days and three final exams later, I was still in Manoa. I didn't purchase my ticket yet. I ignored the barrage of text messages and phone calls from Tyler, which increased when I changed my Facebook page status to "single." I was ready to do some shopping when the letter carrier for our building was stuffing mail into the boxes in the lobby. Aside from all the junk mail, I received a letter from Guam. It was addressed with my full name, Antonia Rae Cruz. The script was wiggly, almost like a child wrote it. I didn't recognize the writing until I looked at the sender's name and address. It was postmarked two days before my grandmother died. The sender's name, *Antonia Q. Cruz* was written in blue ink. I automatically started for the stairs and headed back to my apartment.

I held the letter for about five minutes before I could move again. I looked around my small apartment like I might see grandma sitting in my bean bag chair or glaring at me in the reflection of my mirror. It was sunset and the eerie quiet of the evening didn't help me shake the fear that I might be *mafa'nague*. I sniffed the air for rotting eggs or perfume, remembering stories from my family of being visited by the dead. I sat at the edge of my bed and the envelope, beige from aging was thick and heavy.

I snapped open my cellphone and called my dad.

"Girl! Did you get your ticket or what?" Dad wasn't much for greetings.

"I'm working on that dad. I just finished my last final."

"What the hell? We need your help with the rosaries. The funeral is this Tuesday. *Laña*, girl."

"Dad?" I spoke gently. He did after all lose his mother. "I just received something from grandma in the mail."

I could hear my father's breathing quicken, my twittering aunties speaking in Chamorro in the background filled the silence. I could imagine them in our backyard kitchen, cutting or mixing or marinating food for the rosary.

"When did she send it?" Dad's voice was low and serious. He must have walked away from the relatives since the conversations faded out.

"The postmark is two days before she died, the eleventh." I caught myself whispering too.

"Antonia, you better open it, read it and call me back." My father hung up. I threw my phone on my bed and began picking at the sides of the envelope. This was not the newer self-adhesive envelope. I envisioned grandma with her shaky hands licking this to seal it.

I could see the tattered box of envelopes from the 1990's that grandma kept on her dusty dresser. She stopped needing them for anything more than funeral donations since the parish priest provided pre-marked donation envelopes with parishioner's names--a shady way to keep tabs on who was donating what so it could be listed in the weekly mass newsletter. *Antonia Q. Cruz $10.00*--ranked by the amount donated.

I inserted a plastic knife into the side of the flap. I pushed and ripped through carefully. There were five pages folded haphazardly. The bulk would explain the five stamps. The letter was typed. I smelled grandma's home wafting up from the pages--a mixture of mold, Tiger Balm and flowers. A flood of memories, mostly bad, emerged in my head. I cleared my mind and began to read grandma's letter.

Antonia,
　　I love you. My time is short. You are a good girl. I am happy you are in college. I hope that you are studying. You make me proud. I don't know what you are studying and I should have asked. Your dad cannot even explain it to me. Your mom said its Pacific studies.
　　I also should have bought a calling card to call you. I am very sick. I am writing you this letter because I know how you hate your grandmother. But, I love you still.
　　I hope you realize that you are like a Xerox copy of me. Not only your name, but even your birth month. I was so hard on you, pinching, yelling, smacking you because you reminded me of myself. I didn't want you to turn out like me. I was jealous of you too. You get to go to school.

I didn't. My father was a hard and unloving man, and I am the same way. My father, your great-grandfather Justo, took me out of school when I learned to write my name. He told me that that would be all I needed in life. To learn how to sign my name.

I hope that you and Tyler are doing well. I know he's Japanese and no matter what I say about them, I have my reasons. My father caught me once speaking to a very handsome young Japanese soldier. The scar on my neck, the marks on my back, I can only say that after that day I never looked at another Japanese person again. And, my anger at my father could not be stronger than my obedience. Your father, my wonderful son does not know much of this. I didn't want him to view his grandfather in a bad light.

Your father, well, he did everything he could to help you go to college. He wanted you on Guam, but he knew you were ready to fly. To get out of Guam. I understand. If I had a choice while I was young, I would have been on the first canoe out too.

I was never nice to you. I want what is best for you, so I have set aside a few of my belongings. I know your mother said you want to go to more college. I say go as far as you can with that. Come back to Guam only if you want to, but please take care of your family.

The house that I have lived in for thirty years, although not fancy, is now yours. The land is big and very good for growing. Your uncles and aunties will be mad for a long time at you and me, but I don't care. It's yours to do as you please. Just take care of my orchids girl. They're like my nenis.

The gold necklace with Saint Jude is yours. I hope you remember that I love you and that I'm sorry that I didn't show it more.

Lastly, this is my savings account book and the will I changed last month. I leave the money in my account for your additional college. Again, someone in the family is *going to be pissed off, but you fly with this. The family can fight over the rest of my belongings and the ranch in Piti.*

Your mother is typing this letter for me as I speak. She is a great woman and your dad is lucky to have her. I told her not to tell your dad about this. I wanted it to be between us girls. Take care of mom and dad and your little brother. Family is important and don't wait to be an old lady like me to find that out.

I'll see you at my funeral.

Love, grandma
Antonia Quenga Cruz

Grandma's closing lines made me shiver. The last page had grandma's gold necklace taped on the white paper. It looked like a science specimen. The oval shaped hunk of gold was large and showy, and now it was mine. I ripped open the clear tape, clutched it and started to cry. I opened the savings account booklet. The final balance was twenty five grand and change. Graduate school was in my grasp now. The house in Asan was also to be mine. I couldn't take all this in. I was overwhelmed with guilt and the grief of losing my grandma finally became real. I felt cheated for not having the opportunity to know the real person behind the anger.

I grabbed a duffle bag and stuffed it with several clean outfits. Within ten minutes I was in a taxi headed to the airport.

"So, Toni? What ever happened to the house in Asan?" A mouse of a girl in the middle of the auditorium asked. It was near the end of my first semester of graduate school and final speeches were underway.

My speech tied in my grandmother to the matrilineal lines of property ownership on Guam. I smiled at my classmate.

"It's Antonia, by the way. Well, I let it go."

"Excuse me?" She sat taller and her blue eyes grew wider.

"I didn't want to incite a civil war within my family, so I let it go. The bickering over the land and home started before I even reached the island. My grandmother's children decided to sell and split the profits. Everyone's happy."

"But, you're not upholding the Chamorro custom of passing land through matrilineal lines."

"I am carrying on a different line, an intellectual or academic line for my grandmother. I'll return home to Guam one day to find my own plot of happiness. Besides, my female cousin bought the house."

Another hand shot up in the cluster of graduate students near the exit and I recognized the tattooed arm right away.

"So, did you change your name from Toni to Antonia because you discovered your grandmother wasn't a witch?" Tyler's voice projected. The entire audience turned to him and he blushed, but he kept his eyes steady with mine. My professor had almost a hundred students in her class; she was unaware that the outburst was from a squatter.

"I discovered that my grandma was a strong Chamorro woman who had the fire to succeed, but no path to follow. She was engulfed by her own passion and was misdirected with how she raised her children and grandchildren. Her life came full circle because she realized her mistakes and for that, I have chosen to forgive her and honor her memory. I enjoy using my full first name. Hearing it reminds me of her. Just as my grandmother saw life with new eyes, even if it was when she realized her mortality, I too see everything and everyone with new eyes."

Tyler smiled warmly and held to his lips the raffia bracelet that was once mine.

SAND

Kim dug her toes into the dark sand; the remnants of her pale pink pedicure reminded her of the prior month when she'd had one final bonding adventure with her ten-year-old daughter. Warm morning air drifted through the tent and the Afghanistan sunrise was slinking over the horizon. If she was home, her baby boy, Gus would be nestled in her arms. If she was home she would be listening to the soft snoring from her husband. And if she was home, Ha'ani, her beautiful, doe-eyed daughter would be up watching CNN, worried about her soldier mother's role in the war.

Kim looked around at the weary, but resting soldiers. This would be her family for the next twelve months. She did not want to think about her true family on Guam. She had not found enough strength to pull out the last portrait they took on Easter in Korea. Kim kept it safely tucked in her journal. Kim remembered the day she told her daughter that she was deploying to Afghanistan.

"Captain Mom?" Ha'ani called from the kitchen. "What would you like for breakfast?"

It was Christmas morning in Korea. (Kim was happy her family reunited with her after being in Korea solo for a year). She struggled with the reality that she and her troops could be part of the 30,000 military boost to Afghanistan. It would mark yet another separation from her loved ones. Kim decided to keep her third deployment to herself until after the holidays, and maybe even after they moved stateside.

Kim watched her daughter pull out plates and pans. A fresh pot of coffee was already brewing. Creamer and sugar lined up next to Kim's favorite purple coffee mug. Eggs beaten in a bowl, bacon sizzled in a pan and waffles in the toaster were ready to report for duty. She knew she would miss these savory scents when she was in the desert.

"You are the best daughter, Ha'ani. And a great cook. Grandma and Grandpa would be so proud." Kim tiptoed to kiss the top of her firstborn's curly ebony locks. She didn't want to interfere with her daughter's work stations. She realized that in another year, her daughter would match her in height at the very least. She wondered to herself if she was ever as mature as Ha'ani at that age.

Kim never envisioned being a captain in the Army and a mother of two. She did not see herself ever leaving the safety of her tropical island of Guam. When Kim was ten, she only saw one week ahead of her. She did not have the internet to explore the world and its issues. She did not have parents who sanitized her every thought or move. Kim played in the dirt, she carried on at the neighbor's house until dusk, and she dove into dinner without washing her hands. Today's world, as advanced as it was, was still barbaric. War still existed. Almost thirty-years-old and Kim was an action figure.

"Mommy, I'll wake daddy and get the baby ready for breakfast." Ha'ani's sweet voice pierced into Kim's reverie.

"No, sweetie. Why don't you sit with me for a bit. Let's just enjoy our meal together. We'll wake the boys soon and then rip into our Christmas gifts."

Ha'ani, named after the Chamorro word, "day," sat as directed in the dining chair that Kim patted. She brushed her daughter's curls behind her ear and played with Ha'ani's ruby studded earrings; a gift to her daughter when Kim returned from her first deployment.

"Mom? Are you okay?"

"Yes. Just wondering why you're growing up so fast."

"I am not. I'm only ten."

"Then you'll be twelve, then sixteen, then in college, then a career woman, then a wife and mom. Then ruler of the universe."

"I don't want kids."

Ha'ani's statement nearly rocked Kim off her seat. She never considered herself grandmother material, but the fantasy fluttered in the back of her mind. Before she could absorb her daughter's words, Kim decided to let her explain her position.

"Okay. Why is that, sweetheart?"

"If I'm going to be a captain in the Army like you, I don't want the kids I'd have to leave with their father to be sad. It's hard being sad and away from someone you love. It's not fun worrying about whether they'll be okay. This war has been going on since I was Gus's age, so it might just continue when I'm old enough to join. So, no. No kids for me. Maybe I'll get married when I'm retired at 50 or just get some dogs or travel Europe."

"Oh, honey. The world will be better off by the time you become an adult." Kim said the hollow words and she couldn't reflect the truth in her eyes. She felt like a fraud for saying it out loud, but she wanted to be positive. Ha'ani was exposed to so much of the bad just from the news.

"Will it mom? How do you know? How will any of us know that?" Kim's daughter wasn't being defiant, she genuinely wanted the truth. She wanted her mother to place that heavy, warm security blanket on her and make it stay put. Kim was going on her third deployment. She knew it was hard on her children, but this had become a dream of hers when she finally discovered herself in high school. Excelling in sports and joining the Junior ROTC had been a beneficial move in the right direction. At least that's what her patriotic, retired Army father thought.

"You want the truth, Ha'ani? You're a smart girl. You know why mommy is an Army Engineer. You know why we live in Korea and bounce around every few years." Ha'ani did not break her intense gaze with her mother. "This war may continue for many more years. I am doing my part to better our lives. It's not just the money, it's the opportunity my military career offers. And, I'm not just doing this for our family. It's for American families. It's for those less fortunate." Kim lowered her voice to a whisper and leaned into her daughter's cherubic face. "I haven't told daddy this yet, but next summer, when you're getting ready to start middle school, mommy has to leave on deployment again."

Ha'ani's eyes swelled with emotion. Kim saw her daughter will herself to remain calm and the tears never fell. She reached for her child's hands, still pudgy with baby fat and squeezed.

"Go ahead, mommy. I'm listening. I'm okay."

"I'll be off to Afghanistan this time. I should be able to keep in regular touch. The good news is that you and daddy and Gus will be on Guam for the year I'm gone. So, you'll have Grandma and Grandpa to visit and all your uncles and aunties and cousins." Kim realized that she was saying all of this for her own peace of mind.

"It's not the same as having you with me."

"You're absolutely right, but it sure beats being alone on a military base in winter, right? You do hate the cold."

Ha'ani smiled and Kim imagined that her daughter was envisioning backyard barbecues, Liberation festivities in July, swimming in the warm waters of Tumon and being near her favorite cousins, Isa and Manny.

"It would be nice to wear shorts and tank tops again. And my flip flops." Ha'ani smiled, stood and resumed preparing breakfast. Kim gripped her coffee mug and focused on the swirling cream to keep from losing it.

🐟 🐟 🐟

Kim dug her toes into the nearly white sand. The warmth of the day reminded her that she was finally home. The balmy Guam breeze played softly through her longer locks. The salt and pepper of her hair matched her husband's, and she was glad for the chance to let loose, to relax and not think about military regulations. Her retirement came at a prime moment. Being back on Guam to work as a recruiter and help with Ha'ani's blossoming family and career was a pleasant change. To have a constant was refreshing to Kim.

"Captain Grandma! Look, a blue starfish!" Kim's granddaughter, Penelope, called from her perch at the ocean's edge.

"Penny, baby, don't touch. Grandma is coming." The noon sunshine was dazzling in the child's bouncy ochre curls. Kim lost herself for a second and was transported back in time to when she frolicked on the beach with a toddler Ha'ani. As a young mom, she was more agile then, hopeful about her burgeoning military career. Her crackling knees and the angry knots in her back reminded her that she was nearly used up by the war, but not broken.

"I want it Captain Grandma! Why can't I just grab it?"

"Why?" Why indeed, Kim wondered. Penelope had the same smarts and curiosity that Ha'ani possessed at age four.

"You know what, *neni* Penny? Go ahead. Grab that starfish and make a wish. It's pretty right?"

Penelope stepped bravely into the warm water and reached for the blue star. She held it in the air triumphantly and waddled her way gingerly towards Kim.

"Here, Captain Grandma. It's for you. It's your prize."

"My prize?"

"Yeah! Your reward for being a good Captain Grandma. And for making my Doctor Mommy in your belly one hundred years ago." Penelope placed the stiff blue creature on Kim's white t-shirt, as she laughed heartily at her grandchild's concept of time. The honor surpassed any medal or ribbon she received in the last twenty years of service.

FLIGHTLESS BIRD

The first time Angel walked into Don's Guam History class, her familiar face struck him. Don noticed how the boys, sweaty from playing catch in the courtyard, fidgeted in their seats and eyed Angel as she glided to her desk front and center. Angel was aware of the effect she had on the opposite sex, her usual choice of attire was jean shorts and fitted 80's rock band t-shirts. Her black hair was long, flowing and goddess-like. She played up eyes that were already naturally stunning by adding mascara. A swipe of pale pink gloss was enough to draw attention to her pillow lips. Angel's floral perfume filled the room, which was a welcome contrast to the stink the boys brought with them every afternoon. Don understood fourteen-year-old boys and knew that if he was in their age group, he would be watching her too.

"Mr. Perez? When is our report on the villages due again?" Crystal, the star student of the freshman class asked. The tardy bell had not rung yet.

"Next Friday, and don't forget the interview questions everyone—well, whoever's listening." Don watched as Crystal's gaze went from him to Angel. Angel was fanning herself with a teen magazine, the bronze actor on the cover was shirtless with a cheesy grin. Crystal rolled her eyes and asked Don if he could remove the butcher paper on the whiteboard so she could start copying notes.

"Damn, Crystal. You're such a nerd. Obviously, Mr. Perez isn't ready. By the way, nice tie, Mr. P. Very Dogwarts." John said, a large boy who was repeating the class for the third time.

"Shut it, *Dumb Juan*. And, it's Hogwarts. I'll tell your mom that you're cussing in class, *again*."

"I know what I meant, and I meant Dogwarts!"

"Okay enough you two. Notes in a minute, let me finish attendance and I want to talk about the Chamorro language project we're doing with *Siñora* Aguon's class." Don, fidgeted with the end of his polka dot tie. It was a graduation gift from his girlfriend and she insisted that he wear it. Paired with his fitted short sleeve linen shirt, he felt like a hulking wizarding nerd.

A collective grumble rose from the class of twenty students upon hearing about another project. Crystal was militantly attentive and Angel smiled brightly at Don. This left him unnerved because he had caught her several times in the last week staring at him. He knew it started the previous Friday, when she fished for a compliment. "Mr. Perez, I'm thinking of getting my hair chopped off. Pixie-style." She placed her latest magazine on his desk and leaned over, pointing to a young Disney starlet's do. Don had taken a step back to maintain his personal space.

Don said, "Angel, you would look nice with any haircut, but I like long hair. It's really up to you." He regretted the compliment immediately. Angel kept her hair long.

At the end of the class, Angel remained in her seat lingering over her magazine. Don noticed without looking and cleared his throat loudly as he packed his briefcase. "Everyone have a good weekend. Crystal, don't shut the door, please." She looked again at the empty classroom, save Angel and Mr. Perez. Her face asked Don if she should stay. He smiled at her and nodded dismissively. Don was following the principal's policy. *One student in the room, the door must be left open.*

"Angel. Don't you have to get home?" Angel rose fluidly from her desk and approached him.

"Mr. Perez. I was wondering, since you're still a new teacher and only about eight years older than all of us, why can't we just call you Donald. Or Don, if you prefer." Angel kept her brown eyes on Don's face. She pulled her long black hair forward and continued fanning herself with her magazine. She played with hem of a new t-shirt, Joan Jett's face stretched tight over her chest.

Don's jaw dropped and clamped shut just as quick. The situation wasn't something he learned about in his Introduction to Education course. It wasn't a scenario his mentor, only five years his senior prepared him for. He knew there was a faction of younger, hip teachers who wanted to be called by their first names, but he didn't want to be friends with his students. He knew inside, Angel was angling for something more. Don clutched his tattered briefcase, the one his father gave him when he started college. It had made him feel like a real adult. The room became stuffy to Don even with the door wedged fully opened. Angel seemed aware of his unease, smiled wider and took a step closer to Don's desk.

"What are your parents' names?" Don asked quickly as if he was thwarting an attack.

"Why, *Don*? You're going to call them because of my simple request?" Angel giggled.

"No, just wanted to know if we're related. Guam's so small and all. Because if you're my cousin or something, then maybe you can call me Don, that's only outside of the classroom, outside of school."

"Cool. It's like let's make a deal or something. You're too cute, *Don*. My mom is Analicia Guerrero. My dad is a jerk and I care not to speak about him." Angel's eyes became dark and she furrowed her brows minutely. She stomped out, kicked up the door stop swiftly, then slowly closed the door. She kept her gaze on Don and smiled. Once the door clicked shut, Don exhaled.

As the weeks went by, Angel made her flirtations more public. Don was about to reach the teacher's lounge when Angel reached from behind and covered his eyes with her hands. She was nearly as tall as he was. He could smell her scented hand lotion and her manicured nails scratched his eyebrow. Don recognized her perfume and felt his insides churn, disgusted that he was familiar with her fragrance. He grabbed her hands and turned around.

"Angel! Don't ever do that." Don switched his scowl off to smile as a young choir teacher waited to get into the lounge. He stepped aside and Angel followed his lead. "You're not supposed to be down this wing anyway."

"Oh, Don. Sorry I scared you." Angel then turned to Mr. Lee, the art teacher ready for retirement, as he approached. Don watched how Angel mesmerized his colleague. "Hey, Mr. Lee! You're looking younger these days, sir!" The old man's large smile revealed coffee and cigarette-stained dentures. Don and Angel both flinched. "Have a good day, Mr. Lee. You should really think about my suggestion of dying your hair black." Angel snapped her attention back to Don.

"Angel, you better call me Mr. Perez. Why are you here? Is there something I can help you with?"

"There are many things I can think of." Angel paused to see Don's reaction. He kept his face blank and began to reach for the doorknob. "Kidding, *Mr. Perez*. I just wanted to know if I could interview my mom for the project instead of a grandparent. All of mine are..." Angel acted out a scene of tying a noose around her neck and hanging herself. She stuck her tongue out and rolled her eyes. Don found her disturbing and wanted to escape. He could feel his reputation falling through his fingers just being in her presence. Another teacher passed the duo and even greeted Angel, who didn't acknowledge her. Just the men, Don thought.

"That's fine, Angel. Is your mom willing to come into class for the extra credit? You need it."

"For sure! Maybe you two will click and then you can be my stepdaddy." Angel smiled and glided away. Don felt sweat beading on his forehead. He opened the door and slammed it behind him. The five teachers in the lounge smiled at him except for the math teacher who wiggled her pointer finger at him like he was a small child in trouble.

"Mr. Perez?" Don walked towards the petite teacher in the purple dress, the one Angel ignored.

"Hi. You're new and all and we haven't officially met. I'm Mrs. Angeles." She offered Don an iron handshake. "Don't let a student like Angel get under your skin. Keep it official and she'll get the hint."

"God. You could tell all that?"

"I see you're stressed. Some of these high school girls know how to work it. You just need to know how to deflect it."

Mrs. Angeles must have been in her early forties, but was the type of woman who looked ten years younger than her true age. Don rationalized that she spoke from experience. He whispered, "Do you get the same attention from boys? I mean inappropriate attention?"

"Oh, sure. Boys are just more forthcoming about it. They don't play games, but they're super clumsy. No offense." She smiled. *"Miss, are you married*?" She deepened her voice to mimic a teenage boy. "One kid asked me every start of class for a week. 'None of your business' is an easy response. Try it."

"Yeah, but Guam is so small. Kids have bombarded me with requests to be friends on Facebook. I'm thinking of closing my account, but all my college and Army buddies are on there."

"None of your business means "ignore" button too." Mrs. Angeles laughed. "If things get out of hand, you need to call her parents. Or recommend her to her counselor."

Don felt better prepared to thwart Angel's advances, but there were two weeks of quiet. Don was relieved when Angel missed several days of class. He wasn't tripping up on his words, or deflecting Angel's inappropriate comments during lecture.

The lull ended just before Christmas break. Angel came to class with a shiny red gift box, a large white ribbon adding to its obviousness. She ceremoniously placed the box on Don's desk.

"What's this, Angel?" Don could not keep the anger out of his voice. Crystal perked up and watched them.

"Happy Birthday, Mr. Perez." Angel winked. "I spoke to your lady at the mall. Total coincidence. She was picking out a book for you for your birthday."

"What?" Don's loud voice now attracted looks from the rest of the class.

"Get this box off my desk and follow me." Don ripped the butcher paper off the board and barked instructions to the wide-eyed students to copy notes. He asked the nearest school aide to sit in and he and Angel marched to the counselor's office.

"Oh, Don. Where are we going?" Don stopped and turned to Angel halfway. He did not look at her and decided to bite his tongue. He continued stomping down the empty halls. He held the office door open and pointed to the first chair.

"Sit. I want your mother in here tomorrow."

🐟 🐟 🐟

When Angel's mother walked into the counseling office the next day, Don recognized her immediately. She was the Ana who once pursued his older brother Darren. It caused a big uproar in the family because his father knew immediately who she was when she stood in their driveway.

"*Laña*, girl. You're a Guerrero? You can't date Darren because you're fourth cousins from your grandma's side. And, what the hell are you doing chasing boys. It should be the other way around, girl."

Don wasn't sure he would bring this up. Analicia was his fourth cousin, but not a relative they partied with regularly. Angel was called out of class for the meeting.

"Little Donny?"

"Hi. Mrs. Guerrero. It's Mr. Perez. I wasn't sure if you would remember."

"Of course. You're face is just a good looking as Darren's. How is he?"

"Well, he's still your cousin for one and he's happily married with three kids."

"That's good. You sound so much like your dad." Analicia laughed and Don saw glimmers of Angel in her. "Don't worry, Donny. Definitely not interested like that. Just wondering."

"It's Mr. Perez on campus, please. If we meet at Payless or something, feel free to address me as Don."

"I'm sorry about my girl. She takes after her mother, huh?" Analicia looked at her shoes and twisted the straps of her purse.

Angel was called out of class and her smile faded quickly when she saw her mother and Don seated together in Ms. Cruz's office.

Before Don or Ms. Cruz could speak, Analicia looked at her daughter. "Angel, you know why I'm here. You can't keep doing this thing you do. Leave your teachers alone. It's kind of gross."

"What do you care?"

"I care, sweetie. I want you to think about your future. What do you really want in life?"

"Let's see, I told Don here that I wanted to go to college."

"That's great!"

"But, I also wanted to be a Hooters Girl, then get a job as a flight attendant after I finish college." The three adults looked at each other, but did not speak. Don wanted to tell Angel that she didn't need to go to college to be a flight attendant, but decided her counselor could break the news.

"What about the goal of marrying a teacher?" Ms. Cruz finally cracked the silence.

"Are you serious, Angel?" her mother asked.

"No, not really."

"Well, honey, this is just unacceptable. Anyway, Don, I mean, Mr. Perez here is your uncle." Angel looked at Don and her face twisted. "And, I'll be requesting a transfer out of *your uncle's* class."

"There's no need for that, Ms. Guerrero. As long as she promises to focus on the class and not me." Don said.

"Don't worry, *Uncle* Don. This?" Angel pointed from herself to Don. "Is so over."

There was a collective sigh of relief from the three adults. Angel shifted in her seat, reached up to Ms. Cruz's computer monitor and turned it to herself. "So, Ms. Cruz, can you transfer me to Mr. Santiago's Guam History class, or is he my uncle too?"

GODDESS

I left the movie theater and the warm air engulfed me. It was almost midnight. I was out alone. This was the 67th movie I watched solo. Don't feel sorry for me. This was my own doing. I didn't get to the age of 33, still single, still a virgin, by accident. I am alone on purpose. I am a large Chamorro woman on purpose. My fat is a shield, my armor.

I could tell you the sick details of an uncle who did things to me when I was eleven, or the cousin I idolized who also did things to me when I was a freshman in high school. I'll spare you the particulars. I will say that said uncle is rotting in hell and said cousin is in jail for violating a neighbor's child. I know my past and I know how I cope, but I was ready to fall in love--with myself.

Like the characters in the movies I so coveted, (and I watched anything and everything), the evolution and the rise of a hero was what I wanted. I was ready to slay my demons and start anew. I just didn't want to do it under the sharp lens of my family and friends here on this tiny island of Guam. I was ready to cash out, to go into hiding, to make a dramatic return and live a fulfilled life. I was like a hollow chocolate Easter bunny wilting in the heat. I needed to fill myself.

On an ordinary Wednesday morning, I booked a one way ticket to Washington State. I gave my family two days notice. Not enough time to pretend to plan a going away barbecue. I said I was going to start a new job, which I claimed to have found on-line. My parents knew better than to question anything I did in cyberspace. The most technology in their lives was the television.

The fact was that I was going to a tiny apartment I picked from an on-line service. Pictures had been taken strategically to hide the flaws. I didn't care. I was desperate to start my transformation. I saved money for the last ten years of service at my government job. I cashed out my half of my retirement fund and transferred all my savings to an on-line bank. I had twenty thousand dollars to survive for a year on the mainland. With no one to drive me to the airport, I used a taxi for the first time in my life.

"Where are you traveling from?" the uniformed middle aged man asked when I landed in Hawaii.

"Guam." My voice and posture were already lifted as the miles between me and the island grew.

"Open your luggage." He looked at me, but not my face.

I opened my new black luggage to reveal several sweat shirts and sweat pants, a five pound bag of Calrose rice, beef jerky and unmentionables. I held my breath and hoped that Mr. Uniform wouldn't pull out my excessively large panties. After gingerly pushing things around in the luggage, Mr. Uniform eyed me once more and gestured with a wave of his latex gloved hand to move on.

With a zip, I was on my way to my connecting flight. As I wiggled between the two checkpoint stations, Mr. Uniform said to another agent, "That is one large Guam lady, *brah*."

The crisp air of the Pacific Northwest greeted me. I thought it would smell like Christmas. I should have had a heavier jacket on, but I was fresh off the boat so to speak. I hailed a taxi and offered the address to the chocolate colored man. I was happy he was not conversational. The ride was an hour long, the time I could have zigzagged from *Yigo* to *Malesso'* and back, twice.

The winding road elevated us to a hill. The scenery was a picturesque spring day and the idea that I lived among a forest and not a jungle anymore was exciting. The grand apartment building in brick and white accents was elegant. I loved that it was called Monte Cristo Apartments (being a fan of Dumas's novel and the film). I was a no-income girl and as fate dictated snagged the worse, but only available unit. I read five reviews on-line, four were great and I based my decision on that. On Guam, I had researched the surrounding areas with Google maps and started a list of places I would visit--the children's museum, the library, the naval base and the Kimberly Clark headquarters. I love paper towels. And for cuisine, every country was represented within a three-mile radius. I could have Mexican, Thai or Hawaiian food any day of the week. I had no vehicle, so walking was my only option.

The third floor unit was a challenge to reach and I dragged my luggage up each flight. My exercise regimen started that day. My thighs and arms burned from strain, but it was my rebirth. It had to be dramatic and painful, I thought. No elevators until I dropped at least three dress sizes.

"Aubrianna. You okay, girl?" My mom's voice sounded small on the line, her accent thick. I'm sure she was concerned because I was huffing over the building manager's phone.

"Yes, mom. The flight was fine. My apartment is nice." I didn't feel a pang for my mom or dad. I tempered my fury with them because all that happened to me as a child remained locked in our home. Mom didn't believe me and dad did not stand up to his brother for me. When my cousin did what he did, I didn't bother telling anyone.

"Lock your door, girl. It's not safe out there." I shook my head at the irony of her comment and ended our conversation. I was buzzing to see more of my new place.

Jet lag started to take over. I pulled out two towels and lay it on the floor so I could sleep for a few hours. The unfurnished space echoed. I should have felt lonely, but I felt free. As soon as my head hit the cool floor, I dreamed about the possibilities in my new zip code and I smiled as I drifted into blackness.

"Your usual, Bri?" the cute coffee shop owner asked. I had established some footing in my new town of Everett.

"Yes, Curtis. Make it nonfat though." A month in and I was no longer a 200-pound gorilla. I was now a lithe 190-pound baboon. Progress was progress.

"You still walking and taking the bus?" Curtis asked.

"Yes. I'm liking it a lot, except for the rain."

"Well, if you want a good used car, I'll put a word in for you with my brother. He owns the dealership off Broadway."

"Maybe, kind sir. Maybe."

I took my coffee and the morning paper and sat alone at my usual spot. The sun beat down on my back and warmed me up nicely. I was still not used to the crisp, humidity-free air.

"Ma'am? Sorry to bother you." A deep, honey-dipped voice spoke. I didn't bother looking for the source since there was a more attractive "ma'am" within earshot.

"Excuse me, miss?"

The voice was right over me now. I finally looked up to see a Navy man. His green eyes were locked on my face and I sat petrified. "Me? I'm sorry. Was this your chair?"

"No, ma'am. I just overheard Curtis asking if you needed a car. I'm thinking of selling my old Toyota if you're interested."

I was jittery without having sipped my coffee yet. Feeling bold, I decided to chat with Sailor Austin. His black name tag and many colorful ribbons were impressive. His military haircut was neat and his teeth were picket fence straight and just as white. I felt awkward as he stood over me and I finally pointed to the empty seat so we could be eye to eye.

"I'm sorry. I'm Chief Austin, but you can call me Cade." He sat stiffly on the cushy beige chair.

"Nice to meet you. I'm Bri." His warm hand felt nice in mine as he grasped it firmly.

"Is that short for something else like Britney or Brianne? No, wait. Sabrina, like in Charlie's Angels?" He smiled brightly and I could feel my blood make a mad dash for my cheeks. Aside from Curtis and every other restaurant or café owner in town, I had not had a conversation with a man, a sustained conversation. Comments to cute actors on my television screen surely didn't count.

"Definitely not Britney, but Brianne is close. And, Sabrina, I wish. It's actually Aubrianna." I cleared my throat and held onto my warm coffee cup to remind me that I wasn't dreaming. *Didn't this man have to report to work? And why did I wear my gray 'Hafa Adai, I'm from Guam' sweatshirt?*

"That's a beautiful name. I'll have to Google it to find out what it means." If he'd asked me directly, I would have told him that it was a happy accident of a name when my mom combined the two names she was too greedy to let go of, Aubrey and Brianna. Cade was buttering me up so I would buy his stupid car, I was certain of it.

"Noble, strong, virtuous," I said. "That's what my name stands for according to those baby name sites." He smiled wider. "And Cade is short for Cascade or Cadillac?"

"Well, my parents were militant hippies, so they named me Cadence." He said after he laughed.

This time I smiled. It was a beautiful name.

"I bet your mom and dad have boring names like Peg and Earl." Cade's laughter boomed in the tiny coffee shop and he startled Curtis and the two women there.

"You are funny. My mom's name is Meg and my dad is Carl, so you're real close."

"I wouldn't call that funny. I'd call that creepy."

"Not at all." Cade's constant eye contact unnerved me.

"So, about your car?"

"Yeah, I'm thinking about a thousand bucks. It's a '92 Camry, but I've maintained it and it runs great."

"That's a bit out of my range. Is it stick or automatic?"

"Stick."

"That's going to be a problem. I'm not well-practiced with that."

"Well, Bri, short for Aubrianna. You seem like a nice gal. I'm willing to negotiate the price and maybe even give you driving lessons." I immediately looked at Curtis to see if his psycho meter was going off as loud as mine. Curtis had been watching our exchange like a concerned daddy. I couldn't imagine why this high ranking Navy man was even talking to me. A bell chimed in my ear, that imaginary warning bell that tells me to live it up when my shell begins to harden. I remembered my mission here. I knew that I needed to do things that scared me, within reason. I looked into Chief Austin's jade eyes and smiled.

"Sounds like a good deal. It would be nice to have a car to drive down to Seattle with."

We shook on it and exchanged phone numbers, mine being the front desk of my apartment complex. I was walking on pillows the rest of the day, excited about the potential of this new acquaintance.

⊱ ⊱ ⊱

Chief Cadence Austin was like a nice daydream. It would be another three months before I heard from him again. I filled my time with more walking, since a car sale never happened. I also indulged in furniture, a digital camera, a cellphone, and a laptop--just a few small purchases for the evolving woman. My apartment fit me better everyday.

My first order of business was to establish an e-mail address and a Facebook account. I spent many evenings watching *Ugly Betty* and indulging my voyeuristic urges on Facebook. I saw classmates who got fat, classmates who got hot and those who had a gaggle of children. My list of friends grew slowly. I ignored many too. But, there was one connection that got me excited. Angelica Chong. She was perhaps the nicest friend I had in elementary school--before I hid in a cave, before I ate everything in sight to deal with my misery. I used to sell the chocolate chip cookies my mom wrapped in tin foil to Angelica for a dollar at least once a week. I imagined Angelica as fat as me. Her profile picture was a hibiscus flower, bright and yellow. I felt a twitch in my heart for home, which quickly faded. Her information was privatized, but I knew it was her since all her friends were people I knew. I took a leap and clicked the 'add as friend' button.

"You are gorgeous!" I typed a message to Angelica who added me within five minutes of my request. I didn't even have time to upload a photo, and thought that maybe I wouldn't after seeing her albums. She was a *Chamorrita* Bombshell. We chatted and caught up with our lives. It wasn't until the second night of shallow correspondence that I discovered that she was in Washington State too. She lived thirty miles away. Not much of a drive for Angelica, but a distance for me. We agreed to meet. She wanted to drive into my neck of the woods the following weekend.

"Wow!" Angelica offered me the kind of wow you mutter when you have nothing nice to say. I ignored that. She looked better in person than her photos. I admired how her long black hair shined even in the poor lighting in the back of the coffee shop. Her impeccable make up and style of clothing left me feeling inadequate. Angelica gave me a strong hug and sat across from me, in the same seat that Cade had occupied three months prior. She even smelled sophisticated.

"Wow to you too!" I blurted.

"I'm so glad to find you and in my home state of all places!" Angelica spoke loudly and she vibrated with excitement. She shouldn't be needing any coffee.

"Yeah. I love Washington."

"So, what are you doing out here? Work? School?"

"None of the above." I smiled. "I'm just on an extended vacation from Guam. Trying to figure things out."

"Why Washington? Do you have family out here?" She was leaning forward, still clutching her D and B designer purse.

"Don't we Chamorros have family everywhere?" I joked. I cleared my throat when a familiar voice piped up behind me.

"Bri for Aubrianna?" I knew it was Cade and I saw Angelica eyes widen ever so slightly. And from the way her lips curled into a flirty smile, I knew she would want an introduction. I maneuvered myself to turn and face Cade. He was in civilian clothes and looked ten years younger. His green eyes still piercing, but the blue plaid shirt fit his physique like it was painted on. He looked like a farm boy model who walked right out of a catalog; all he was missing was a piece of straw dangling from his lovely mouth.

"Hi, Cadence, I mean, Chief Austin. Or, Cade!" I was carrying on like a nervous chicken.

"Cadence? I love that name!" Angelica stood to shake his hand. Cadence wasn't lost on Angelica's exotic beauty as he took a lingering look at her. But, then he turned his attention to me.

"I'm so sorry that I didn't get to call you back in May, Bri. My ship pulled out all of a sudden because of that disaster in Indonesia."

"Oh, you don't need to explain. I've been fine without a car."

"You look great! I mean, it's been three months and you look different." He smiled. "A good different."

I had lost another twenty five pounds, but I was still wearing the same sweats. This time I had my University of Guam sweatshirt on in a hideous hunter green. It was nice that he noticed. I was both glad and sad to see Cade go. I relaxed my face when he turned to leave. He promised a phone call on the weekend after I gave him my new cell phone number. He offered a tour of his ship, including Angelica as an afterthought it seemed.

"Wow, girl! You know how to pick them." Angelica bubbled.

"Pick what? My boogers?" I joked. "Cade is just a Navy Chief who offered to sell me his car."

"He's into you. I saw it." I then remembered why I liked Angelica so much. She never took anything from me without paying.

※ ※ ※

"I am not wearing skinny jeans when I don't fit into that size category." I spoke through the flimsy gray curtain that separated me from Angelica. She had taken to being my fashion and fitness mentor in the last month--her little pet project. Angelica threw a pair of jeans through the opening and ordered me to put it on. I checked the tag and it was marked size 12. Six months earlier on Guam, miserably shopping--I was a size 22. There was no way in half a year I shrunk that many sizes.

"Bri, don't make me come in there and spank your *dagan*! Put the damn jeans on and get your butt out here."

I slipped my right leg in the jeans and then the left. I knew the floor wasn't large enough for me to lie down and squeeze in. I pulled the waist up slowly, dramatically. I closed my eyes and sucked in my tummy as I attempted to zip this corset for my bottom half. It was like I left my body when I zipped up effortlessly, then fastened the button. I exhaled loudly and found that I was comfortable in a size 12. I tested the pants further by doing a full squat. It didn't suffocate me and the button didn't fly off. I threw open the curtain dramatically and posed. My arms held the frame of the doorway.

"I told you, Bri! You look amazing. You've must have lost another ten pounds since last month. Now, for a sexy top. We have to show off all of that!" Angelica gestured to my chest area. "Cadence is not going to know what hit him tonight. I'm so excited to be your Hairy Godmother."

"I just can't believe this will be my first date. Ever."

※ ※ ※

It was five in the morning when my mother called from Guam. Cadence reached for my cell phone before I could and he answered in his deep voice.

"It's your mom." The mom who didn't know I had a steady boyfriend for the last few months.

"Hey, mom."

"Aubrianna?" Who else would have answered with 'Hey, mom'? I wondered. "Who's that man?"

"Don't be concerned with that mom. What is it?"

"What do you mean, 'don't be concerned'?" she challenged.

"I mean, I'm 34-years-old and a grown woman. It's early mom and I have work this morning. What is it, please?" Cadence rubbed my back to calm me.

"Your cousin, Victor. He's dead, girl. Suicide. Hung himself. You need to come home."

>=< >=< >=<

Cadence held my hand as the plane touched down on Guam. It would be his second trip to the island, but his first via plane. He took the last of his leave, fourteen days, to be with me. To help bury my cousin. To help me bury the past. I had not been home in a year. I had not kept my finger on the pulse of the island in a year. Aside from calling my mom and dad on their birthdays, I created a tourniquet between my past and my now.

At the airport, the humidity hit me hard and I was glad that Cadence arranged for a rental car. Here I was returning to Guam, a stronger woman, but still fragile about my past. My history with my cousin Victor had set me off on a path of destructive behavior. I would have imploded if I didn't find refuge in Washington.

We headed straight to the Navy Lodge. I didn't tell my parents my flight information. I didn't want them waiting at the arrivals lounge, fidgeting, uncomfortable—pretending they cared to see me. They wouldn't have recognized me anyway. And, they wouldn't have believed that Cadence was real, that a man of such beauty and heart would ever really love me. He did. He was there before I rose from the ashes.

Cadence wanted to physically harm the men who molested me as a child, but they no longer existed. He cried the night we almost consummated our relationship and I panicked. He held me tight as I explained my torture and my escape to Everett. Cadence and I had yet to reach that level of physical intimacy, but emotionally—we were already there. We had been together for six months and he promised to never push me. I believed him.

I made it through Victor's funeral by becoming numb. Numb like the evening I knocked on my family's door. The night they realized that I was not the same Bri who left the island. After Victor's funeral, my parents were updated on three facts: one, I had a job and was training as a travel consultant with Angelica's firm and two, I was happily in love, and, finally, their dear nephew, Victor had molested me three times.

I left the movie theater and the cold Washington air embraced me. It was almost midnight and I was out with my fiancé. This was the 18th movie I watched with a date. You can feel happy for me. This was my own doing. I didn't get to the age of 35, engaged and still a virgin, by accident. I am a Goddess on purpose. I am a beautiful Chamorro woman, on purpose. My fat is no longer my shield.

YES, I AM.

The black Honda Civic crunched angrily on the white gravel driveway. The cherry stained closet doors of the open garage appeared before Sirena had time to slam on the brakes. Balding brakes that should have been changed five thousand miles ago. With the echoing of metal colliding with wood, Sirena's rattled father flung open the screen door to find his sixteen-year-old daughter hunched over the steering wheel. He nearly ripped off the small car door, ignoring the extreme heat of the window frame caused by the car baking in the sun of the high school parking lot. His baby sobbed uncontrollably as Ted's nervous and frantic hands wiped away her sweat drenched hair, looking for the source of her pain. There was no blood. He became aware that Sirena was wearing a different, more revealing top than the blue t-shirt she left to school in, but decided to let it slide. The splintered wood of the doors he painstakingly stained, varnished and installed himself lay on the concrete ground. It was the first project he undertook when his wife died five years ago.

"Sirena! What happened? Look at the goddamn closet doors! And the car!" Ted's gruff booming voice was not what his daughter needed right now and he knew it. His temper flared only after digesting that she was physically fine. Teenage emotion was a foreign realm to him and he didn't want to *go there*.

Sirena raised her puffy eyes to her father and a flash of her now ex-boyfriend's face appeared before her. She shivered and heaved when it dawned on her that Gene looked like her dad. A fresh wave of hatred surged. *The closet door? The old, Guam bomb? What about me?* Sirena did not argue back, her upbringing taught her that her angry father's questions did not require answers.

Sirena attempted to push her father away, but that would be like pushing on a concrete wall. Ted was over six feet tall and almost three hundred pounds. His build made people assume he was a linebacker. Solid through and through. Sirena's grandfather always said, "Too bad Guam doesn't have an NFL team." He was nearing forty, but his chocolate complexion and Army regulated haircut made him appear ten years younger.

"Where do you think you're going, girl?" Ted followed his daughter into the home, both happy for the cool, air-conditioned relief.

"Dad, I don't want to talk about it please. I'll pay for the doors and the car."

"With what?" Ted knew how she would answer.

"With the money mom left me!"

"That is for your U.O.G. tuition! You better stop trying to use that account!"

"I don't want to go to college on Guam! I want to leave to the mainland or even Korea! Maybe I'll join the Army! I hate it here and I hate," Sirena stopped herself before putting the final stake in the coffin. She knew it wasn't her dad's fault that Gene dumped her. Gene was the quintessential Chamorro boy. His family had a ranch. He drove a lowrider truck he tinkered with himself and he smoked like his life depended on it. Gene was über-islander and she was not. Gene's attraction to Sirena was that she looked like the many beautiful Japanese tourists in Tumon. He never told her that since he knew she was sensitive about not being brown enough, her Asian eyes like ethnic billboards. He was also relieved that Sirena wasn't possessive like his last girlfriend. Gene was secretly happy Sirena was book smart and he liked and respected her dad. They spoke in Chamorro the few times they met, often joking at Sirena's expense, since she was mute to the native tongue.

"Sirena." Ted spoke more calmly. "*Maila halom.* Tell me what happened."

Sirena let the doorknob to her bedroom untwist with a squeak. Pulled by the strings of obedience, she turned around slowly to her father. Realizing that she was wearing a revealing red top, she pulled her long black tresses forward and wrapped her arms around her waist. Finding the furthest possible spot on the couch, Sirena kept her eyes hidden from Ted. Her line of vision settled on her mom's picture in a cheap silver frame. Her omma's smiling eyes and delicate pink lips were from the same picture used in her funeral obituary. Sirena choked down her tears and wished she had her omma next to her to tell her that Gene was a fool. She would tell Sirena that the jerk didn't know how special she was and that she could fall in love again.

"Did something happen with Gene?" Ted asked. Sirena raised her angry brown eyes to her dad and he gasped at the intensity in her young cherubic face.

"What about, did something happen to me? Forget Gene!" Sirena wielded her words like an expert swordsman.

"Wha- what happened?" Ted decided to stop guessing. He didn't want to squeeze lemon juice into whatever wound was inflicted on his daughter. He longed for his wife at that moment and his eyes flickered to Young Hee's picture.

"Gene dumped me. His mom said I wasn't. I wasn't Chamorro enough and she doesn't want Oriental grandkids, like they would be pieces of furniture." Sirena's shoulders slumped and she deflated before Ted's eyes, while a category 5 super typhoon brewed in his chest. His hand began to reach out to Sirena's shoulder, but he dropped it to the couch. Ted had a short list for why Gene was satisfactory for his daughter, but race was never a factor. Ted fought hard for his family to accept Young Hee as his wife and if Gene couldn't fight for his daughter, he didn't deserve her.

"Dad! How many letters in the Chamorro Alphabet?" Sirena asked from her bedroom. It had been three days since she crashed the car and broke up with Gene and she hoped she was forgiven by her dad.

"*Sa, hafa?*" Ted asked *why* in Chamorro. He cringed at the sound of his teenage daughter's voice as it ricocheted in their small, air-conditioned home. It reminded him of Young Hee at times.

"I have a stupid alphabet book project for my Chamorro class!"

Sirena's father's heavy footsteps clopped through the Gumataotao home as he was determined to whip respect back into his only child. Ted grabbed a tattered Chamorro language reference book off his desk and bee-lined for her room. He counted to ten before appearing in the doorway. He wanted to maintain peace this week. There were no locked doors allowed in this house and his blood bubbled in his skull when he thought of Sirena speaking to him like he was her peer.

Sirena Ha'ani Lee Gumataotao was born in South Korea a year to the day after Ted and Young Hee met for the first time. Ted was serving his fourth and final year in the Army and with the addition of a wife and child, he was more than ready to fly home to Guam. He named his daughter after the Chamorro mermaid legend of Sirena. He added *Ha'ani*, meaning "day" for good measure. Ted did this before it was in vogue culturally to name your child after a Chamorro term. If he had a son, he would have named him *Rai*, meaning king.

One child was all his petite wife could handle; the birth of Sirena almost killed her. Although his daughter held the Chamorro name, her face betrayed her heritage. Sirena had daily battles in elementary school with children who looked more "islander" than she. Her delicate features, jet black hair, almond eyes and milky white skin were beautiful to her parents, but strange to her classmates.

"Dad? What's a Japanese?" Sirena's question plopped on the dinner table when she was in the second grade.

"Why do you ask, *neni*?" Ted kept his face calm as he assessed the stress in his child's face.

"The kids at school keep calling me that and they won't play or share with me. Is it an alien? I thought I was Chamorro and Korean and American." Sirena's bubble gum lips pouted minutely. She tried her best to keep a strong poker face like her omma taught her.

Ted held his daughter's small ivory hand in his. His skin was the color of enriched earth and with his child's hand enveloped in his, the stark contrast of their appearance was evident. Ted provided a textbook explanation of Japan and its people and Guam's history with them. Sirena took the information in and it settled in her seven-year-old brain. She resumed eating, so Ted looked to Young Hee to see if he handled the situation correctly. His wife filled Sirena's bowl with more rice and filled her glass with more water and without looking at Ted retreated to the bedroom.

The house grew still after dinner. Ted gently pushed Sirena's bedroom door open. He slowed his breathing and watched his wife sitting on the pink princess toddler bed. Three story books lay at his wife's feet, having been consumed for the evening.

"Sirena. Did you know that every person is different? Skin is like the cover of a book. One is different from another, but each contains a beautiful story. Did you know that you are a gift to daddy and omma? You have a story within you. You stay strong when people say bad things to you. Maybe they are just curious about you. You are unique and beautiful, my princess."

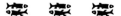

Sirena was eleven when her mother was hit by a drunk driver. Omma insisted on walking everywhere. She was walking to the village's mom and pop market for Ted's Marlboros. It was a Monday morning and the sun barely peeked in the horizon. Balmy air marked another routine day. Ted agreed that he would get Sirena up and ready for school if Young Hee bought him his daily pack of cigarettes. That was the last day Ted smoked.

Sirena was sixteen when her father died. Lung cancer ate away at his bulky frame. The demon nestled in his body for months before he admitted he had a problem. The morning Sirena was ending her junior year and stepping into her senior year, Ted passed away. Sirena weighed more than her father and nearly lifted him off the hospital bed when he breathed his last breath.

Sirena longed to leave the island and worked hard to save money, working at her uncle's Liberation carnival booth for a chance to attend college in the mainland. The eve of her senior year, Sirena received a death benefit insurance check and her dream of leaving Guam was granted.

Sirena stood in line at the Guam Club's monthly fiesta. She followed the directions on the bright green flyer she yanked off the student announcements board at San Diego State University. She had made it through one semester away from Guam. The longing for home, her relatives and cousins and Chamorro cooking struck her hard during finals. The scent of fried fish and coconut milk drenched bananas wafted through the courtyard. She eyed the large aluminum tin filled with red rice and her mouth immediately flooded with saliva. Finding the end of the line, a J.D. Crutch song with an upbeat tempo made Sirena sway happily and it helped her keep warm. It was sixty five degrees, toasty for a California winter, but cold to an island girl accustomed to eighty five degree weather year-round.

The food line was a hundred people long. Sirena didn't realize how many Chamorros there were in San Diego. Although she saw the occasional SUV with a Chamorro Flag or latte stone sticker, she had yet to run into someone who grew up on Guam. Sirena felt at home as the Chamorro language was spoken all around her. She closed her eyes and imagined that her father was still with her, picking up on some of the conversation, getting lost in most other utterings.

Sirena had met a Chamorro boy in her math class, but he was raised in Sacramento and had never been to Guam. She felt a little sad by that. Corey had very little interest in Sirena's ranting about island life. Although he loved to wear the latest tribal designed sweater from the Fokai collection of Guam and wave the shaka (hang loose) hand gesture, which was actually Hawaiian; he had no clue about living the Chamorro culture. She attempted to ask him to this fiesta, but his glassy eyed expression during their last billiards game made her stop. She decided to not let him win for once.

Sirena never wore her heritage on her sleeve, despite her appearances dictating that she should. She had grown steadily proud of her Guam roots in her senior year in high school. This was initiated by the fact that her father died before summer break. Many of her dad's siblings, all eleven of them, worried that she wouldn't make it through to graduation, being officially orphaned. Sirena worked through it with the help of her dad's eldest sister, Beck and her favorite first cousin, Rose. Auntie had seven children of her own and invited Sirena to live with her by joking, "As long as you're potty trained baby doll, you can live with me."

Infused with a sense of belonging, Sirena decided to snap a picture on her cellphone to send to Rose on Guam. Someone with a leaded finger tapped her shoulder. A Chamorro man, who could have been her father's age, scanned Sirena up and down. His face was steely and his dark eyes unwelcoming. Sirena respectfully waited for his response, half thinking that he might speak to her in their native language, but she thought the better of it, looking more like Lucy Liu than a Chamorro girl.

"Hey, girl. Are you from Guam?" The man's eyes did a once over again. Sirena wore a gold Guam seal pendant around her neck, her bon voyage gift from her godmother. It grew heavy all of a sudden and Sirena felt like ripping open her feather down jacket Superman style to display proof that she was from Guam. Sirena's eyes fought tears as the deep tone and the Chamorro accent flowing from this interrogator mirrored her late father's voice.

"Yes, I am. *Hafa Adai*!" She greeted him as best as she could with the phrase she taught some of her friends in writing class for a presentation a week before.

The man sneered and asked, "What's your name?"

"Sirena Gumataotao."

"You married to Chamorro?" Another question shot at Sirena. His voice rose one octave.

"No. My dad is Chamorro." She wondered for a second if she should have said *was Chamorro* since he was dead--resting peacefully next to her mother at Whispering Palms Cemetery. At that moment, she wanted to have red dirt shoveled on her as well.

Still not satisfied, the man asked what village she was from and her family name. Both of which she answered precisely. Another man in a red hibiscus island shirt, cologne announcing his arrival, walked by and told Sirena's interrogation squad of one, "*Laña*, Vic, don't hit on the tourists!" He winked at Sirena and said, "*Konnichiwa!*"

A flood of shame and anger burst upward from Sirena's gut. She was sure her white cheeks burned red. She turned to the table and questioned if it was worth staying. She wanted to yell, *"I am not a Japanese tourist!"*

The smells of home cooking compelled her to remain in place and the ingrained custom of respecting your elders pinned her tongue in place. Sirena made it to the fiesta table without another round of questioning, but she became more aware of people analyzing her. She kept her line of vision down and piled her plate modestly, despite the grumblings of her empty stomach. She even skipped her favorite dish, shrimp kelaguen, since her interrogator hovered over the pile of pink yumminess.

Sirena walked to the bar for a drink. She decided she would eat in the car and then head straight to her apartment.

"*Hafa adai!*" Finally, a warm voice welcomed her from behind the bar. Every older woman reminded her of an auntie back home. The raspy voice from decades of smoking and the Chamorro accent gurgled out of the sixty-something year old woman's mouth. Sirena smiled warmly and thought that maybe she would stay. The Paraiso Dancers from Guam were scheduled to perform later in the afternoon after all.

"*Hafa adai*." Sirena declared. She wanted to tell the nice matronly woman serving iced tea that she was from the village of Asan too, since many of the Guam Club members wore nametags emblazoned with their home village.

Before Sirena could continue, "Auntie Sita"—as marked on the nametag said, "Girl, there's a sauce called *finadene'* at the end of the bar. It's got onions, pepper, lemon juice and soy sauce. Just put it on your rice and meat. People from Guam love it!"

"Oh, really?" Sirena's voice shot out louder than normal. "Well, I am from Guam. I am Chamorro. I am from Asan. And, I know damn well what *finadene'* is."

Finding refuge in her roommate, Raquel's Prius, Sirena looked over the plate of food. She flung her napkin wrapped fork and spoon on the passenger's seat and grabbed a shrimp patty with her fingers. The first bite should have been wonderful, but the oily fried mush felt foreign in her mouth. Maybe it did need *finadene'*. Sirena covered her food with an extra foam plate. She watched the club grow smaller in her rearview mirror as she navigated her way home. At the first stop light, she offered the warm plate of food to a homeless Navy veteran.

"Thank you sweetie! Red rice!" His eyes bulged and he smacked his lips together. "I've been stationed on Guam! *Si Yu'os Ma'ase*!"

"You're welcome." Sirena offered as the light turned green.

Sirena hit her second semester running. She fed her need to belong by joining writing groups and enjoying the sights of San Diego. She got a city bus pass and trolley card. When she wasn't studying she was visiting museums on the rotating free days, running 5K's and meeting new people. So, when Raquel invited her to go riding in the sand dunes of Yuma, Sirena was already stuffing her back pack.

In a circle of perfect strangers, the campfire glowed and mesmerized everyone. S'mores and beers and soda circulated amongst the group and animated conversations echoed in the sandy fantasy land. Sirena sat quietly enjoying the pop music in the background. Her cool Coke sat half full by her feet. She wondered if her dad would be happy with her path. She knew her omma would be impressed that she kept her chin up and was meeting new and different people. Sirena met and remembered everyone's name in this makeshift tribe.

A large white, Ford 350 made an appearance in the distance. The plume of sand it kicked up was beautiful as it obscured the setting purple and pink sunset. Someone in the circle said, "There's Robert! Wasn't sure he would make it."

Sirena was thankful that Raquel's family's fifth wheel had all the comforts of home. She ducked away before the new guest arrived. When she returned, Robert was in her seat. Viewing the back of his head, he was easily the tallest amongst the group. His wind whipped brown hair was attractive and Sirena was suddenly curious about his face. She always found it fascinating when someone's profile or back side didn't match the front side.

The sand shifted to accommodate each step she took. Raquel hit Robert's arm, "That's my *chica's* seat. You're a gentleman, right? Move!"

Just before Robert turned around, he said, "If she's cute, she can sit on my lap."

Sirena stopped and her feminist's side, infantile as it was, became angry. Robert laughed and stood up to see whose seat he stole.

"Oh, sorry! I'm sorry." Robert repeated. "Here!" He pointed to her seat. Robert crouched down and grabbed Sirena's bottle of pop. "Is this yours? I'm sorry!"

A few of the ladies in the circle giggled, while Raquel rolled her eyes at her cousin. He stumbled backwards, nearly tripping over a large rock that lined the campfire. Raquel's parents, Rich and Clare laughed heartily.

"I've never seen you uncoordinated son," Rich stated.

Sirena blushed and she felt warm; not from the campfire, but from Robert's obvious frazzling, and perhaps in part because of his crystal blue eyes. Before she realized it, everyone in the circle made a space and a blue fold up chair appeared to her right. Robert ran his hands through his hair and approached Sirena. His gray shirt fit him well, revealing an athletic build. He smiled the biggest and toothiest smile Sirena had ever seen and gestured with an open palm to the chair.

"May I?" He asked.

"Sure. Just don't expect me to sit on your lap." Sirena stated. Robert cringed and his cheeks flashed crimson. He smiled and sat stiffly next to Sirena.

Raquel engaged Sirena in conversation about their literature class. Sirena listened with her other ear at Robert's conversation with his aunt and uncle. There were plans for one more day of sand dune fun before heading back to SDSU. Several campfire members called it a night. Raquel winked at Sirena.

"This is the cousin I said was in the Air Force." The statement didn't ring a bell for Sirena. "The one who's been to Guam?"

"Oh, yeah!" Sirena barely recalled the conversation she had with Raquel when she shared her disastrous day at the Guam Club six months prior.

"Well, goodnight, kids." Raquel mimicked her parents' comment and added, "Be good!"

"So, Robert, you've been to Guam? How did you like it?" Sirena expected Robert to say it was boring and hot.

"Um, I loved it there. I hope to go back."

"Would you have guessed I was from Guam?" Sirena didn't let him answer. "Most people think I'm Asian or something, which I partly am."

"No, I would have known." Robert smiled. His chiseled face softened in the firelight. "You look like an islander to me."

※ ※ ※

Sirena had in her heart the confidence to walk into the Guam Club a year later. She had in her mind a shift in perspective. She had in her soul the pride of culture that couldn't be suppressed.

Sirena held Robert's hand and led him through the archway held up by large gray *latte stones*. Robert inhaled the savory scents and lowered his lips to Sirena's ear, "I hope they have *latiya*, and I hope it's as good as your recipe."

Finding their place in the long line for the fiesta table, Robert held Sirena in his arms and they swayed. Robert sang along with the Chamorro love song blasting on the speakers. Sirena turned to her new boyfriend, wide-eyed.

"I told you. I know Guam, and I loved it there."

The elderly couple behind Robert and Sirena smiled at the couple.

"Excuse me, doll." The small Chamorro woman in a vibrant pink-island print dress addressed Sirena. "*Auntie Liang*," her nametag identified, with Asan in bold blue letters. "What village are you from?"

"My family is also from Asan." Sirena was happy that she wasn't interrogated about her ethnicity. "Familian Gumataotao."

"Oh, my! Are you Ted and Young's girl? Auntie Beck told me you were attending school here. Sirena?"

"Uh, yes." Sirena smiled and in a flash found herself being embraced fully by the little lady. "*Sa*, I'm your Auntie Liang Gumataotao Hartley." She proceeded to explain the branches of the family tree. Sirena beamed. Her new found auntie held her hands in hers. She surveyed her niece's face. The purity of her skin, the depth of her brown almond eyes and the character of her face were undeniably her mother's. "Didn't you yell at the irritating lady offer at the bar last year? *Ai*, girl. I was right behind you. I thought to myself, that little girl's got gusto. Maybe she's a Gumataotao. You left so quickly, my little old legs couldn't catch you." Auntie Liang laughed loudly.

"Well, I'm happy I found you auntie." Sirena held her auntie like she found a long lost teddy bear. They feasted together like they had been acquainted for years. This time Sirena's plate teetered in her palm with a mountain of food. The Chamorro dishes prepared by the many contributors sang on her tongue with every bite. Robert stroked Sirena's long black hair, watching her glowing face.

"My sweet Sirena. Are you enjoying yourself this time?" Auntie Liang asked, resting her wrinkled perfumed hand on her niece's cheek and winking at Robert. Sirena looked from Robert to her auntie. She smiled.

"Yes, I am."

APOSTLE'S CREEP

Twelve creeps at the dinner table *with Jesus Christ.* That's what Isaiah thought his Sunday school teacher said. Apostle's *Creep*. It was a prayer that he couldn't memorize entirely. Isaiah's throat felt like the desert while his palms became moist every Sunday as he knelt. He would clasp his hands in prayer and the words escaped his eight-year-old mind. Isaiah did well with the first half of the prayer, but once he reached, *"He ascended into heaven,"* a fog set in his brain. He moved his lips and dropped the volume of his voice. He tried his best to catch up with the recitations of the group of twelve students.

Isaiah was an only child. His father was rarely home and when he was, he smelled of sour sweat, cigarettes and beer. His mood matched his scent and he never wanted to be bothered, especially by Isaiah. Mother was hard at work at the middle school and Nana was too impatient to practice the prayer with him. The television was his best friend.

"In two weeks, each of you will recite the Apostle's Creed in front of *Pale'* Mike." Ms. Pier said. Isaiah liked his new *Eskuelan Pale'* teacher, but he hated when she asked them to do projects.

"Do we need to say the 'Our Father' or 'Hail Mary' too?" asked Jayda.

"No. Just the Apostle's Creed. You all should know those two basic prayers perfectly by now."

"What happens if we mess up? Can we start over?" Julienne asked next.

"I'm sure *Pale'* Mike will allow you to start over. But, please, we want to do well. How about for every student who does well, you can pick stickers from the prize box?" The girls cheered, while the four boys in the class groaned. Most of the stickers in the prize box were for girls, with only a few race cars. Isaiah and the other boys had two of everything already. It wasn't enough of an incentive for Isaiah.

"Do we have to do confession again?" Isaiah's voice was as meek as a mouse. He didn't usually speak up. He always felt that God would strike him down or send a lightning bolt from the sky directed at his *dagan;* at least that's what his Nana had told him.

"Yes. Glad you brought that up. After class today, *Pale'* Mike will be waiting for our class. So think about what you have done that is not so nice this past week." Ms. Pier smiled.

In Isaiah's mind, a parade of misdeeds played like it was on T.V. On Monday, he took two cookies from Nana's stash in her room. On Thursday, he paid the nearly blind cashier at Buzz's mom and pop store two pennies, instead of two dimes. And just before class, Isaiah said, "God doughnuts" so he could impress his older cousin. His stomach churned as he wondered if he had to tell *Pale'* all of his sins.

"If we did five bad things, do we need to tell *Pale'* Mike all of it?" Jayda asked again, somehow reading Isaiah's mind.

"Yes. Just tell him everything. It's like emptying your basket of bad things. *Pale'* Mike will give you penance and the Lord will forgive you, no matter what." Ms. Pier reassured.

No matter what? The words hung in the musty air and Isaiah decided to test this theory. He told his three misdeeds in detail to the priest. No thunder or lightning. Isaiah even saw *Pale'* Mike smile slightly like he was amused. After saying his five Our Father's and three Hail Mary's, Isaiah felt lighter and wondered what he could get away with in the next week.

"My child, Isaiah. How are you this blessed day?"

"I'm good *Pale'* Mike. May I begin with confession?"

"Well, of course. You've thought about everything you've done?"

"Four things. First, I kicked my neighbor's puppy because it kept licking my foot. *Not hard though.* Second, I took three cookies this time from Nana's cookie jar. Then, yesterday I pushed my classmate, Ray because he called me a roofus. *Not hard though.* And fourth, I, um, I took fifty cents from my mom's wallet to buy gum."

"Is that all?"

"Yes, *Pale'* Mike. That's all. I'm sorry."

"Well, for this next week, think about what you're about to do before acting. That's the best way to keep the Lord in your heart. *Esta,* you are still a good boy. Now do five Our Father's and five Hail Mary's." Isaiah noticed that *Pale'* Mike did not smile throughout his confession this time, but more importantly, he realized that a giant electric bolt of lightning did not strike him dead.

"Isaiah, my son. I hope you had a great week. Ready for confession?"

"I was born ready."

Pale' Mike frowned. "Where did you learn that phrase, boy?" Isaiah flinched at the tiny flash of anger from the young priest.

"I, um, heard it on T.V. Is that a sin? Watching T.V.?"

"No, my child." *Pale's* face softened. "Let's not use that phrase again. Please begin."

"Ms. Pier said it wasn't a sin, but I didn't do well on my project of memorizing the Apostle's Creep, yet."

"The Apostle's what?"

"Creep?" *Pale'* Mike searched Isaiah's face to see if he was joking and smiled when he realized the genuine misunderstanding of an eight-year-old child.

"*Ai, adai*, Isaiah, it's Creed. d, d, d. I expect you to know it by next week, huh?"

"Yes, *Pale'*. Apostle's Creed, duh, duh, duh." Isaiah sat forward like he was about to tell an exciting story. "I have four things again this week. First, I took four cookies from Nana's jar." *Pale'* Mike clapped his hands together and bowed his head.

"Isaiah, does Nana know you're taking her cookies without asking?"

"I don't think so." Isaiah lowered his eyes and his cheeks grew rosy. "I won't take anymore from her *Pale'*." The young priest relaxed his hands on his lap and nodded his head for Isaiah to continue.

"Second, I called Julienne a roofus when she bumped into me." Isaiah looked out the arched windows for signs of dark clouds and continued confidently when he saw only cotton puffs floating by. "Third, I poured my dad's beer in the sink when he fell asleep. Last, I took a dollar from my mom's purse so I could buy a Pepsi."

Isaiah watched the priest and noticed that he was a lot darker in complexion than he was. He wanted to ask what his last name was, remembering that Ms. Pier had said that he grew up in the village. He wondered if the *Pale'* and his teacher were the same age. Isaiah considered being an alter server, but thought that since he couldn't memorize the Apostle's Creed, that he wasn't good enough. *Pale'* Mike looked at Isaiah intently and shook his head. For a moment, the priest's gesture reminded him of his father.

"Isaiah. It seems that every week, your misdeeds get worse. Are you testing the Lord?" The child's flushed face and averted eyes told *Pale'* Mike what he needed to know.

"Ten Our Father's. Ten Hail Mary's. Now, go."

Fear moved Isaiah to his designated pew. He knelt on the olive green kneelers and began his prayers. Isaiah pulled out ten coins from his pocket and laid them out. He always wondered why his pennies smelled like blood as he rested his face near his folded hands. He recited the easy prayers from memory. After each prayer he moved one penny to the completed pile. Ms. Pier smiled as she monitored the praying children. Only Jayda had nothing to confess for the week.

"Okay, *Pale'* Mike will be taking confession today, but he only has thirty minutes. He is heading to Saipan with the confirmation class for the week, so think about the one thing, the most major thing you want to confess today." Ms. Pier said.

Isaiah had only one thing to confess. His final test to see if God really did punish bad kids like his Nana said.

"Isaiah. How are you this weekend?" *Pale'* Mike smiled his half-smile like the Jesus in the large painting in the foyer of the church.

"Good."

"What do you have to confess this week? Remember, just one big thing."

"I only have one thing, *Pale'* Mike." The priest tilted his head and regarded the baby-faced Isaiah.

"I didn't steal cookies this week or push anyone. I didn't say a bad word."

"That's good, my son. Continue."

"*Tan* Gertrude. She lives near the bridge."

"I know *Tan* Gertrude." *Pale'* Mike's voice was tense like the taut jump net firefighters hold open, ready to catch someone escaping from a burning building. His wide eyes told Isaiah to continue.

"I was at her house with my Nana. They were playing cards. She has a nice house. It has air-con. And it's bigger than mine. The garden is nice too." Isaiah was the last to confess that day. The priest's patience was melting. He knew the young child was nervous. And the priest was fearful of the escalation of sins from Isaiah and what he might hear.

"Isaiah." *Pale'* Mike pointed to his watch. "Please."

"I went to her wallet and took this." Isaiah reached into his jean pocket. The pants were a size too small. He pulled out two wrinkled one hundred dollar bills. *Pale'* Mike stood, grabbed Isaiah firmly by his arm and walked him to the side exit of the church. He pushed open the glass door and escorted Isaiah towards the Sacred Mary Garden. The heat and humidity of the noon air hit Isaiah in an angry blast. He squirmed in *Pale'* Mike's steady hold. He knew he was wrong and his eyes instantly searched the bright sky for a thunder cloud. Maybe *Pale'* was going to bring him to the street so the lightning bolt could have a clear target, he thought.

"Nooo." Isaiah said.

"No, what? Isaiah, I am very angry with you."

"I'm sorry. I was going to return it today. I just wanted to tell you what I did. I wanted to know if Jesus would kill me."

"What?" *Pale'* Mike relaxed his hold on the child and crouched down to look at him at his eye level. The priest's voice was less bristled. "No, Isaiah. Jesus won't kill you. But, if you ever steal from anyone, ever again! I am going to kick your butt for Jesus."

Isaiah's eyes went wide and tears glistened in his baby browns. "My Nana says it's true, that Jesus will get me if I'm bad. I just wanted to make sure I was safe."

"Isaiah. You cannot live your life doing bad things just to see if you get punishment. *Tan* Gertrude is my auntie. You cannot be taking things from people, even if it's cookies from your Nana or this…" The priest held the bills in front of Isaiah's face. "…two hundred dollars from a kind, old woman who needed it for her food and medicine."

"I'm sorry." Isaiah's lower lip pouted.

"Well, Isaiah, you must want to grow up to be a lawyer or scientist. Evidence. Very smart, you are, but you do not test your loved ones or God or me like that. You are a good boy and good things will happen." *Pale'* Mike relaxed his shoulders and wiped the sweat off his forehead with his linen handkerchief. "I apologize for getting angry."

"It's better than my dad or Nana getting mad at me." Isaiah wiped his nose and eyes on the back of his arm. *Pale'* Mike nudged Isaiah's shoulder in the direction of the glass door. Ms. Pier was watching curiously from inside. *Pale'* reached for the door as kindness settled back on his face.

"Your penance will be ten Our Father's and ten Hail Mary's. Then, you will walk to *Tan* Gertrude's home and return this." Isaiah quickly placed the wrinkled bills in his pocket. "You must apologize and let her know you confessed. Lastly, I expect you to be able to recite the Apostle's Creed, *duh, duh, duh* next week." They both laughed.

Taimanglo

"Yes, *Pale'* Mike." Isaiah looked up at the young priest and smiled. "I won't make you mad again. I don't want to disappoint you."

"My child, just don't disappoint yourself."

Isaiah sat in the blue folding chair in front of Ms. Pier and *Pale'* Mike, his muddy black sneakers an inch from the floor. He felt his classmates' stares warming the back of his head. Isaiah had volunteered to be first. He folded his hands in prayer, took a deep breath, focused on the crucifix above *Pale's* head and began. *"I believe in the Father Almighty, Maker of Heaven and Earth . . ."*

CHIRIKA'S PEPPER PLANT*

A lively breeze traveled through the Salas home, taking up the scents of grandma's afternoon cooking. The sweet smell of bananas and coconuts and homemade sugar doughnuts made its way to the backyard where Chirika was picking hot peppers. Chirika ceased her humming when the attractive odors captured her attention. She quickly picked the last of the peppers and raced inside.

"Nana, are the doughnuts ready?"

"*Ai*, Chirika," her grandma replied, "you always seem ready to eat, but never ready to help." Grandma smiled as she checked on the fresh bananas simmering in coconut milk.

"I'm sorry, Nana, but I wanted to collect the *donne'* for tonight," chirped Chirika.

"Well, I'll make you a deal. You help me clean up and I'll let you sample whatever you want, *esta*?"

Chirika's grandma always made her special desserts on the weekends.

She tried to make enough to last the entire week. Chirika's mother enjoyed taking snacks to work, since she was always too busy to cook anything on her own. She worked at the high school as a secretary and she also had a weekend job as a salesclerk at the supermarket in *Agat*.

Chirika knew she lived a simple life. She had a simple home and family comprised of her mother, her grandma and herself. She had no brothers or sisters, but her numerous cousins filled the void for her. Chirika also knew from an early age that her father had "gone on a mission" with the military. She had not seen him since she was three-years-old.

For Chirika, the most vivid memory of her father was when she had stepped on a rusty nail. She could clearly remember her father as he cradled her in his arms and carried her home. She felt safe. The pain from the puncture on her right foot seemed hardly noticeable at that instant. The throbbing pain returned because her father said he would bring medicine to help it heal. Her mother wiped Chirika's forehead with a wet towel and whispered in her ear to keep her baby girl calm. Her father returned to the room empty-handed, or so Chirika thought. She looked for the medicine he said he would bring, and she thought it would be some pill or serum to swallow, or liquid to wipe over her wound. Her father knelt by her foot. He held something small and red in his fingers and squeezed what felt like fire into Chirika's wound. The pain radiated throughout her foot, into her toes and up her leg, fortunately stopping at her knee. She wailed because the pain felt one hundred times stronger than when the nail had pierced her foot.

Sometimes, Chirika would rub the small scar on the bottom of her foot and remember her father. Through the years, it was beginning to smooth out and she was afraid that as the scar disappeared, the memories she had of her father would fade away too. Fortunately, it was Chirika's mother who kept his memory alive through her stories.

"Mama, can you tell me again about my Papa?" asked Chirika sheepishly.

"Chirika, how many times do you need to hear this story?" asked her mother, regretting the remark as soon as she made it. She could see in Chirika's eyes that her daughter needed to hear the story. So, like many other nights, she sat on her daughter's bed and began the tale. It was a tale of a man who seemed foreign to her life experience. She was numb to the magic and emotion that her daughter was absorbed in every time the story was told, but she told it nonetheless, staying true to every detail . . .

Papa's eyes were a deep, dark brown and his hair flowed like silky waves. His skin was a golden brown which could easily turn a deep chocolate if he worked under the sun. Your Papa was a tall man, but he never looked down on people. Instead, he was very helpful and respectful to the elders.

Maybe that's where you get your gentle eyes from, Chirika.

I met your Papa when he moved into the house down this street. He didn't grow up on Guam, so being here for the first time was both scary and exciting. We were seventeen-years-old. We met in the church choir. I played the flute because I was a horrible singer. Your Papa, on the other hand, had the most beautiful voice in the tenor section that our village ever heard.

I think that's where you get your love of music from, Chirika.

Many girls at school claimed that they were in love with your Papa. They went out of their way to get his attention. You would have thought Elvis Presley came to Guam. I remember a girl named Lea who made fresh titiyas every morning for him. Another girl offered to help him with his homework. That was your very own Aunt Carmella.

Fortunately for you, your daddy didn't fall for any of their tricks. Who knows who your mother might be right now, Chirika?

Your daddy and I were good friends during his first year here. We taught each other things—I taught him how to plant, cook and sew; he taught me how to swim, carry a tune and drive a car.

As friends, I wasn't your Papa's first choice for the senior prom. As a matter of fact, I wasn't even his second or third choice. First, your Papa asked Jenny Meno. She declined because she was dating your Uncle Tomas. Then, he tried to ask Julita Perez, who said yes. They soon found out that they were third cousins. They called it off immediately, but the family continued to tease them about that for a long time. After the kissing cousins fiasco, your Papa decided to ask a girl from outside the village. He thought it would be safer. Her name was Andrea. She lied about her age, so when he found out she was only fifteen-years-old, he canceled the date.

You may be wondering why your father had such a hard time finding a date if he was such a "stud" in the village. Well, your Papa was no long-term planner so he asked these girls the week before the prom. This was a time when dresses were being made, tuxedos were rented and flowers were being ordered. Your Uncle Kin was the man in the village to see because he created beautiful dresses and flower arrangements with the help of his wife and daughters. So, Papa's quest for a suitable date and outfit seemed hopeless.

Too bad for your Papa, it was me he finally had to ask. I can remember him turning to me in math class and asking me to do him a favor. I thought it would be something simple like sewing a hole in his jeans or helping him pick donne' to sell. Your Papa sure did love that spicy food. His favorite dish was freshwater shrimp kelaguen in hot corn titiyas. It had to have a lot of donne' or it just wouldn't taste right for him. He loved it when his eyes watered and his ears popped because of the pika taste. I just couldn't handle too much donne'. I'm more of a sweet tooth.

I think you get your love for *pika* foods from your Papa, Chirika.

Anyway, after class your Papa pleaded with me to attend the senior prom with him. He didn't want to call it a date, but a favor for a friend.

I told him that I didn't have anything nice to wear and he said that he would help me sew something nice. The idea of getting a new dress for my very small wardrobe was tempting. I couldn't resist, so I said yes.

Prom night came and went. I didn't feel like it was anything special, but after that night your Papa sure acted weird around me. I noticed he would start stuttering or sweating a lot when we would spend time together. In class, he barely said "hello" without a quivering voice. I just couldn't understand why he was being so mamalao around me until one of the girls mentioned that he was in love with me.

Me! I couldn't believe it, Chirika.

I thought of him more like a brother than a boyfriend. The news of this made me nervous also. I tried to avoid him so I wouldn't stutter or fumble in front of him either.

It took almost a week after the prom for your Papa to even speak a full sentence to me. He asked if I would be interested in a drive-in movie, instead of our usual swimming lesson.

See, Chirika, we used to have a drive-in theater down here, but many parents did not approve of it. It was later shut down.

I told your Papa that I wasn't allowed to go to that place, so he quickly came up with Plan B and asked me to the bowling alley on the military base. I had never tried bowling, but I was willing to learn. Papa explained to your grandma what bowling was, but when he said that the balls were around ten pounds each, Nana refused. She did not want me carrying any load heavier than ten pounds because she thought it would ruin my chances of bearing children. Papa reassured her that I would only use the seven pounders, so she agreed. Nana told him to have me home by ten o'clock, and Papa, being a gentleman, had me home thirty minutes early. Nana really like your Papa then.

Our journey as boyfriend and girlfriend was a sweet and simple one. It was not as complex as the ones you see on T.V. or in the movies. We had one or two dates a week, which usually ended by ten. He visited some weekday evenings, never empty-handed. Sundays were the most fun because we spent the morning at mass, and then later had brunch in the social hall. Our families always enjoyed each other's company.

After two years, your Papa and I were married. Papa wanted to quit working at his father's feed store and join the military. I was interested in the idea until I discovered I was pregnant with you, my angel. Papa loved the idea of being a father, so he abandoned joining the Army for saving money for your arrival. When you were born, your Papa's eyes shined like I had never seen before. He would just hold you and watch you breathe, commenting on how beautiful his daughter was.

Our lives were great for the next few years. When you were two, your grandpa closed down his feed store and decided to return to the States. That left your Papa here with you and me and Nana. Papa was upset because that would mean losing his job. He was even more furious that his father did not offer to give him control of the store. For the next year, Papa tried every job from working for a farmer to cafeteria duty at the high school. He continued to love us, but his dream of joining the Army came back to him. He even went on a diet to be lean enough for the weight requirement. That was when I knew your Papa was serious about leaving. I decided that I was not going to take any chances with our money situation. Food was scarce for us and I did not like depending on your Nana all the time. I looked for a job at the high school, offering to take over Papa's job in the cafeteria. Nana agreed to watch you during the day. Your Papa signed up without talking to me any further. He said he would finish boot camp, get stationed near his mom and dad in California and then send for you and me.

Unfortunately, as soon as your Papa's training was over, he was whisked away to a foreign land, somewhere in Asia. I received one letter from him, promising to send for us as soon as the war was over. So, you and I and Nana have been waiting ever since.

"Chirika, your father loved you. You know that?"

"Yes, but . . . if he loved . . . never mind, mama. I'm tired."

"*Esta*, my angel, you rest. You have school tomorrow."

That evening, Chirika dreamt about a man and woman. The woman lay on the sand, lifeless. The man was tall and seemed to be radiating light. He emerged from the ocean. He looked like the sun rising in the morning. The man stood over the woman's body for a moment and then suddenly bolted into the village.

By Easter break, Chirika's mother had fallen ill. The family doctor called it a heart ailment, perhaps the same one that killed Chirika's grandfather who had passed away when her mother was twelve.

The doctor reassured Nana that all mother needed was rest. They ordered her to take a month off from work, since the stress would be a burden on her health.

While Chirika's mother recuperated at home, they spent a lot of time together. Chirika, being her inquisitive self, learned more about her mother than ever before. There were stories of childhood adventures, both good and bad. Also, Chirika truly understood how her mother felt when her dad died. She realized that she shared a lot in common with her mother.

On the eve of summer, Nana found her daughter lifeless in bed. Chirika was resting on a cot in the corner of the room, as she had for the past month. Chirika was awakened by Nana's screams.

Before calling relatives or the hospital, Nana, with Chirika by her side, recited the rosary.

"Chirika, parents shouldn't outlive their children. Your mama is much too young to be in heaven." Nana said that evening. "I really feel that your mother died because of a broken heart."

"What do you mean, Nana?"

"You know, your mama was still very much in love with your father.

In the last few weeks of . . . her life, I often found her writing something. She would never tell me what it was."

Nana's rough hands stretched out to Chirika. In them was an envelope. Chirika held the sealed letter tightly as her eyes studied the names. *TO: General C.J. Guerrero FR: Mary Ann Salas Guerrero.*

"Chirika, I think your mama was writing to your father because she knew."

Chirika folded the letter and shoved it into her back pocket. She wasn't sure if she should mail it or read it. She did not want to think about it just then.

Later that evening, Chirika's Uncle Tomas knocked on their door. Nana answered it while Chirika was asleep on the couch. She was half awake and could hear her uncle and Nana conversing in Chamorro. Chirika understood some of the conversation. She heard that someone was in a car. A visitor.

Chirika's curiosity got the best of her and she leaped from the couch to the screen door. She could see Nana hugging someone. The man was very tall, with neat hair and simple clothing.

Something in Chirika's chest began to tingle as Nana escorted the man to the door. Chirika perched herself behind the kitchen table, suddenly remembering the letter that was bulging in her back pocket.

"Chirika, *sigi magi*. There is someone here to see you."

Chirika walked up to the stranger with confidence.

"Hello, Papa."

The man was shocked that she would remember him. He reached out his hand to shake Chirika's. With a firm grip, she shook her father's hand.

After dinner, Chirika asked Nana if she could show her father their garden. Nana realized that the girl wanted time alone with her dad and sent her off. Nana could see something familiar in Chirika's eyes, something reassuring.

In the garden, Chirika bombarded her father with questions. He answered questions about his life, his adventures, his accomplishments and most importantly, his intentions on Guam. Her father was taken aback at her confidence and intelligence. Chirika stood next to a *donne'* plant and looked at him intently.

"Papa, this is the plant that Mama taught me to grow." chirped Chirika. "There are many things that you don't know about my Mama and I'd like to be the one to tell you about it."

Chirika's father carried over two hollow concrete blocks to sit on. He was enchanted by Chirika and was eager to hear her tale.

"Mama was a sweet tooth." commented Chirika. "I think that's where I get my love for desserts from. Mama was a hard worker and maybe that's where I have learned my many skills. I also think that I inherited my Mama's nose and hands. There are many things within myself that are gifts from my Mama."

"Chirika, I, I am so sorry for," stuttered her father.

"Papa, my Mama died of a broken heart. She still loved you. I am not sure if I have the same love for you, but I am willing to give you a chance, if you choose to stay." Chirika said as she reached into her back pocket for the letter. "This is Mama's last letter to you."

Chirika's father took the letter from his daughter and kept her hand in his. In his eyes was the promise of love and commitment.

Author's Note: *Chirika's Pepper Plant was first published in Guam in 1998 as Latte Magazine's Short Story Contest Winner.*

THE LIST

"Each of you must bring a gift in proportion to the way the LORD your God has blessed you." **(Deuteronomy 16:17)**

"Where the hell is the *chenchule'* list?" Tata yelled from his bedroom. My uncle's viewing at Santa Teresita church started half an hour earlier. Tata needed to know how much my Auntie Louisa gave us last year. This was not how I wanted to spend my Saturday morning, but this was Guam. Funerals are a local past time.

I rummaged through the contents of my desk for the tenth time. A stack of last semester's college papers cascaded to the ground adding to the confusion. I cursed myself for not keeping better records. Scraps of paper, receipts, and index cards peppered my floor. Mom was always great with filing, but she's dead. Living the life of an angel up there somewhere, not worrying about who paid what or who gave what dish for a funeral or birthday. I was not trained in the art of *chenchule'* documentation and I was suffering for it. I did remember that my *nina* wrote a bad check for ten dollars once and Tata paid a twenty-five dollar returned check fee. Who the hell writes a check for ten dollars? Tata stopped talking to her for two years after that.

I tried to channel my psychic energy, and I hoped my mom would put the exact amount in my head. I'm sure I could make up a figure and Tata wouldn't know the difference—but, Auntie Louisa would. *Ika*, more specifically, is a serious matter on Guam—you give, you get back equally.

"*Hafa*, Cassidy, what's taking you so long, girl?" Tata was at the door, his only black dress pants fit looser since mom died. His waistline shrunk, but his rotund beer gut did not.

"Damn, get a shirt on Tata. You look gross!"

"You better hurry up! The viewing is almost over! And, for your information, *Tan* Ana thinks I'm dead sexy." He shuffled back to his room.

The church was a minute drive away and viewings were several hours long. We could walk there, but the sun would burn us to a crisp like vampires. That didn't seem so awful; anything to get out of this vicious hunt for a list and yet another funeral. It was my fifth funeral that summer.

I began to sweat and wished Tata wasn't such a penny-pinching crazy man. He shut off our air-conditioner every morning at ten. "Too much power! We're just making G.P.A. rich." He would prophesize.

The tank dress I wore didn't keep me cool. I continued to forage around my room on my hands and knees when my *dagan* knocked my dresser and the hot curling iron I set on the edge fell and burned my back. One howl later and Tata asked, "That better be a scream because you found the list!"

Climbing to my feet, I stomped to my door and yelled back, "Fifty freakin' dollars! Fifty woohoo bucks, Tata! Let's go already!" I guessed high and I'm sure Auntie Louisa would appreciate it. Tata came to my door again, now fully dressed.

"Girl, borrow me *fan* fifty bucks. I'll pay you when I get my check. And, I need an envelope. And, write my full name and yours. And, don't forget the village."

At the church, I was thankful for the air-conditioning. I dodged the usual nosy cousins and the usual creepy uncles. I averted my eyes and remained behind my father as we followed the procession of people ready to stare at my uncle's lifeless body. It was nice to see him in a three piece suit. Navy blue looked good on him. I glanced at everything but my uncle's face. My dad's eyes glistened a bit. I wondered if he feared his own mortality. I did.

"Dad, why didn't they put uncle in his favorite Budweiser shirt?" I whispered.

"Hey, Cassidy, *shaddup*," Tata pinched me without anyone noticing. "Anyways, it's right there by his leg." Folded neatly, next to a can of beer, were my uncle's favorite things.

Tata made a big production of kissing everyone in the receiving bench, even the men. I followed his lead. As he handed Auntie Louisa the pale lavender envelope, he made it a point to tuck it in her hand dramatically. He should have placed it in the *chenchule'* box next to the large yellow bouquet from Senator Babauta's office. Tata may as well have done a James Brown twirl, since he wanted the gift to be noticed. As I watched their exchange, I knew I wouldn't see the borrowed fifty dollars again from Tata.

I followed Tata to the social hall where he complained to his cousins about his gout, all the while munching on *fritada*. Nothing like pork and guts simmered in blood for brunch. I wanted to get home to clean the typhoon of paper in my room.

"Tata, I'm going to walk home." Too happy to be among his cousins, Tata dismissed me with a nod of his head.

The quarter mile walk was not so wise. My neighbor's dog was loose and I had to do some fancy running. Brownie didn't get to munch on my leg since Mr. Taitague yelled from the kitchen window; his gruff command like an invisible leash yanking the dog back to the carport. At least I got a workout in that day.

At home, I started up the air-conditioning. I placed my glass of iced tea on my dresser and decided to start organizing my life. I categorized each slip of paper, index card, receipt and greeting card in nice piles on my bed. If I didn't get through the mess, I would be sleeping on the couch. After an hour of sorting, I finally found the pink sheets of paper where I wrote the names and donations for mom's funeral. I narrowed my eyes and scrolled down the list. I found Auntie Louisa's name. I collapsed on my bed and all the neat piles I created migrated to me like I was a magnetic force. A whoosh of air exploded from my lips and I looked at Auntie Louisa's name again. In my handwriting was *Auntie Louisa Reyes (Mangilao)--$5.00 (cash).*

SKIN TAG YOU'RE IT

"**Grandpa! What's *dat?*" Hunter pointed to** Jose's shirt, or so he thought.

"What's what, my grandson?"

"That *ting*, those *tings*!"

"It's 'things', Hunter, not 'tings". *Sa hafa*? I got a bug on my shirt? Are there green onions in my teeth?" Jose laughed heartily. Hunter hopped off his booster seat and walked to his grandfather's side of the brunch table. He stopped eating his cookie to investigate, so Jose knew this was serious.

Sunday brunch for the Aguigui family was a tradition. Same restaurant, same table, same meeting time after mass. The view of the beach in East *Hagåtña* was beautiful. Hunter was nearing three-years-old and was very authoritative and as curious as a monkey named George. He was Jose's only grandson in a kingdom of seven granddaughter princesses.

Hunter grabbed his grandfather's floral printed shirt by the sleeve and pushed it up over his bicep. His grandson's eyes widened with delight. It seemed like slow motion to Jose as Hunter's right pointy finger reached up to touch a large bulbous, fleshy skin tag. Jose quickly pulled his sleeve down and his three sons with their similar laughs broke the quiet in the restaurant.

"*Laña, neni* boy. You better go back to your seat and finish your food." Jose used his serious tone. Hunter was persistent and tried to push the sleeve up again.

"Grandpa! What is *dat*?"

"That's my twin brother." Jose laughed.

"Honey, don't tell him that!" Lillian said. She smacked her husband's shoulder playfully, while he wrestled with his grandson to keep the growth on his arm hidden. Jose had it for the past ten years. *Nothing to worry about,* his doctor once said. *The technical term for a skin tag is acrochordon or fibroepithelial polyp. Removing this would be purely cosmetic.*

"Hunter, my brother won't like that very much!" Jose watched the strong child's line of sight shift and Hunter grew still. He was now gazing at his grandfather's neck. Jose knew instantly that Hunter was looking at the darker and smaller skin tags that dotted his neck. He waited for the reaction. Hunter climbed on his grandfather's lap expertly and yanked the shirt open, nearly popping the top button off. He rested his pointy elbows on Jose's full belly.

"Grandpa! What's all *dat*!" The child's face pressed close to investigate more of his grandfather's skin.

"Is that your brother's little army?" Jose's youngest son said.

"No, that's evidence that dad loves to eat too much Spam!" The elder son declared.

"No, it just happens. Half of all people get it. I bet all of you have at least one." The middle son stated. Jose always liked his middle child.

"The key is to find them when they're small and pinch them off." This time Lillian addressed the table. "Auntie Edna ties floss on hers and cuts the blood circulation. After a week, it shrivels up and falls off."

There was a collective gasp of disgust from everyone. Jose's pretty daughter-in-laws placed their forks on their plates with a synchronized clank. Hunter remained on his grandfather's lap tickling his neck.

"*Neni* boy, you need to finish your food. Now." Hunter hugged his grandfather and slid off Jose's leg.

"Okay, grandpa. But, what are *dats*?"

Jose lowered his voice and told his grandson, "These are my black diamonds. I don't need to buy any jewelry since I have these." Hunter seemed satisfied with that explanation and returned to his seat and nibbled on his cookie.

Upon Hunter's fourth birthday, he was enrolled in preschool. Jose signed in at the desk and showed his identification to the young lady, like he had for the past week. His robust grandson bolted from the back of the room when he saw his grandfather waiting to take him home.

"Grandpa! I beat the snack timer today and got a sticker! Look!" Hunter danced and waved the arm with a red rocket sticker.

Hand in hand, Hunter and Jose headed for the exit, maneuvering around ten other four-year-olds playing and carrying on. Hunter stopped and pointed to one of the teacher's assistants.

"Hey, Grandpa! Ms. Gosseling has diamonds!" The pretty teacher's aide with a round face turned and smiled at the pair upon hearing her name.

"Oh, she has a nice diamond ring?" Jose whispered.

"No, grandpa. She has diamonds on her neck like you! Except, they're pink!"

THE TIGRESS CLUB

My name is Zen Machida. I lead an elite group of female athletes called The Tigress Club. Once a week, I meet with them on their turf. We discuss old times and upcoming challenges. They teach me everyday about strength and what it means to be a real woman warrior.

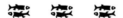

"I call this meeting to order at 2:13 P.M. this fine Thursday, May 5th, 2050." My voice traveled throughout the conference room as the fifteen women settled in and sat at attention. They were fine specimens at their golden ages. The youngest of the group was my auntie from Guam, Calily Quitugua. She celebrated her 88th birthday and my gift to her was heading The Tigress Club of San Diego.

"First order of business is the Rock and Roll Marathon on the Moon next month." I pounded my fist on the silver podium to draw the attention of a few talkers in the back. The centurions sometimes got distracted by their tattoos and fight tales. I had just noticed that the three ladies had their heads wrapped in silk.

"Sorry, Madame Zen." Graciela spoke for the trio. "We were just so excited about the upcoming marathon that we did something drastic for the race."

It was grilled in me to respect my elders and the three women were like giggling high school girls. I couldn't resist and gave them the floor. They still had the physiques of athletes in their fifties and were more than capable to run the twenty six plus miles of this race. Graciela, the eldest at 107 years-old, pulled the women at her sides up on their feet. We were all captivated as they ceremoniously unraveled their silk turbans in blue, purple and pink. The radiant women smiled as there was an audible reaction, then applause from the floor.

"Wow, ladies! I'm honored." Their hairdos were cropped short, like mine, but more amazing was the bright hues they dyed their hair. Graciela stood proud with her electric blue spikes. Martina ran her fingers through her fluffy purple crop. Alicia swayed side to side like a child as we admired the pink flames on her head.

"When the hell did you guys do that? And who authorized it?" Auntie Calily was not chastising the trio. Her tone relayed awe.

"We did it this morning with the help of Alicia's granddaughter. She's a stylist and she did this pro bono. You guys like?" Graciela addressed the other Tigresses. Hoots and cheers followed.

"Okay, ladies, gorgeous job. We should have no problems tracking you during the race." I passed around my portable scanner. Each lady scanned their right heel. Their imbedded chips transferred all the necessary information I would need for the race application.

"Second on the agenda is an upcoming cage fighting seminar. Aside from myself conducting clinics, we have invited some of my teenage students to serve as sparring partners. I'll need to know which of you ladies need to order more gear or workout clothes. Zap me an e-mail." I wanted to keep on our one hour schedule, but I expected many side conversations. One, two, three. A toned arm shot up on my right. Bridget's Japanese koi tattoo wiggled from the strength and enthusiasm of raising her arm. I nodded at her.

"I apologize, Madame Zen. Didn't you say you were going to be bringing some of those beefy MMA fighters you know? I would like to grapple with them." Some of the women giggled, but the applause made it clear that these Tigresses, although in their golden years were still warm-blooded beasts craving the touch of the opposite sex. Many of the ladies have had husbands that they've outlived or divorced. I smiled and checked my notes.

"Well, Bridget I did promise that. I am awaiting confirmation on two people. My father should be able to come in from Brazil. Then, Journey has yet to confirm."

The women began whispering excitedly to each other. More than one of these women had Journey's or my father's posters in their rooms. Although the two men were young enough to be their sons, I was afraid of the touch-fest that was going to undeniably occur.

"Lastly, ladies, if we can control our dwindling hormones, I have the recommended surgeon who specializes in tattoo enhancements. Dr. Woo handles celebrities and is doing this as a favor to me. We can start scheduling appointments, pro bono after the marathon."

"Does he do tattoo tightening? My pixie is looking a bit droopy." Lani, the former women's professional boxing champion asked. Before I could answer, another Tigress asked a question.

"Recolor, too? And the band above my ass has got to go! It has my third husband's name and I want it off." Joan, the newest Tigress to the group asked.

"Ladies, all of that can be taken care of. We'll discuss that next week. Now, this weekend after breakfast, I'll meet all of you in the gym for some weight training." I said. "Dr. Woo's business card should be uploaded to your laptops by now. Let's adjourn the meeting please."

After I hugged each of the Tigresses, my Auntie Calily walked me to the foyer. She still dressed in her best designer clothes. Today, it was a lavender pantsuit. She was always such a beauty. Her four-inch heels clicked in the hallway and she held onto my arm. "Thank you again for hanging out with me and my *kaduka* friends."

In the Chamorro culture, a place like this for our elders was typically out of the question. "Auntie, I plan on retiring from fighting in three years. Then, I really want you to move in with me up in L.A. You can work at my gym."

"Oh, *neni*. This is my home. I couldn't leave the other Tigresses. They need me." She smiled warmly as we reached the front door. "I'm kind of a big deal, you know."

"Yes." I laughed. "You are pretty awesome, Auntie. I'll see you this weekend. No high heels in the weight room."

>=< >=< >=<

My name is Zen Machida and I volunteer at The Tigress Nursing home.

ECHOES
(For my Father)

The night my dad died, I sat at the edge of my parents' bed until I heard my mom's whispering and weeping turn into gentle snoring. My seven-year-old son slept next to her in the spot his *Tata* once warmed. After his second stroke, they moved in with me for help. It was my duty as a daughter and I was happy to offer my home. My husband was on his fifth deployment and we had been blessed with being stationed on Guam after almost eight years in the mainland.

"Everything for a reason, neni," my dad used to say. I believe that more now, but I'm angry. Angry that God took my father away. I'm angry that I couldn't hold my last pregnancy. Angry that my husband was not by my side when my father expelled his last breath. Angry that Tano had to see his grandfather in the physical state he was in at the ICU and then at the hospital morgue. *"Mom, why does Tata look so different? What are those needles? Why can't he hear me?"*

I wandered in my home, the cold tile reminding me that the evening was real, I wasn't dreaming. I had lost my father at sunset.

I wanted to hear his voice again, feel his rough hand on mine. I reached for the seven brown prescription bottles on top of the refrigerator. My limbs felt weighed down by cinder blocks as I made my way to the sink. I emptied each bottle that was supposed to sustain dad's life for the six months the doctors promised. The pink, blue, white and yellow tablets looked like candy. I ran warm water over the pile of pills and watched the medicine's colors swirl and combine into a cloud, as my mind filled with the memories of the last week.

Dad seemed strong in his last three days. He actually wanted to go to the hospital for his appointments. He willingly ate the medicine I placed on the dining table next to his bland meal. He requested some of his favorite dishes and even though it was bad for his health, mom obliged. The smells of *fritada*, barbecue *tataga'* and *buñelos aga'* filled the house. Dad nibbled at each dish, unable to hold much down. His body had withered, his eyes were sunken in, but he seemed more like his old self.

My cellphone blasted my favorite song telling me that my husband was calling in and it dragged my mind back to reality. I desperately wanted this to be a nightmare I could wake up from.

"Hi, Vance." My voice sounded foreign to me.

"Hey, Trinity. How are you holding up?"

"I want you here."

"I know. They're working on getting me home in three days. I'm sorry." The line went silent and I heard him sniffle.

"Got some sand in your eye?" His giggle made me feel better momentarily. "How are you honey?" I asked.

"I'm fine. Just remembering pop, that's all. We were supposed to work on building that… and now, I don't have anyone to turn to for construction advice. I miss him."

Telling Vance about rosary plans and the funeral home details made the reality of dad's death sting fresh. Many things I had to decide with my mom consulting. I still had to secure a *techa*. It's not something you would look for in the yellow pages under "rosary."

"I'm glad you can make it back for dad."

"I don't want to leave my squadron, but it would kill me if I missed saying my final farewell to dad."

><> ><> ><>

The next nine days were like hurdles that I didn't have enough breath or energy to jump over. Mom smiled at everyone and only wept quietly on our drives home from the church every night. Tano sat near my mom and held her hand, honored by his latest responsibility.

"Mom, do you want to live with us? Permanently, I mean?"

"No, Trin. I'll be fine. You're dad. Our house." I knew what she meant.

"Grandma, you can move to the states with us next year. California is nice." Tano said bouncing in his seat. It was the first time I saw mom smile since before dad died.

"I'll see if Tata wouldn't mind. We'll talk about it later. Your own dad has a say in this too." Mom wanted to consult my dad about moving? I couldn't imagine how I would react if Vance died.

"Mom, you know Vance won't mind."

"Are you sure?" Mom and Vance did not see things the same way at times. Although they wouldn't admit it, they were of the same fabric; headstrong, in control of their feelings and stubborn. Vance always teased that mom would have made a great soldier.

Taimanglo

Beads of sweat dotted my forehead and the eighty-eight degree heat and humidity pounded on the one hundred mourners. Vance held my hand as my dad's gray casket was lowered by three husky teenagers who looked like brothers. The United States flag had been folded neatly and presented to my mother. The women and children placed red and white carnations on the casket in farewell. Vance had tied his pallbearer ribbon on the shiny handles of the coffin. There was a flurry of people saying more condolences after the last gospel song was played. Some rushed to their cars for air-conditioned comfort, while others hovered around my mom and me. Vance had been home for five days. He needed to head back to the war in two days. As I held him, I inhaled his scent, one I had known since our junior year. I relished in the thought that in five years, he could finally retire and we could live on Guam permanently. The vibration from Vance's phone startled me. He released me to take the call. I watched him under the shade of the canopy, my father laid to rest just feet away from him. My husband hunched over then dropped to his knees. Vance's mother and those nearby rushed to his side. I ran to my husband and dropped to the warm grass.

"Vance! Vance, what's wrong? Are you okay?" I thought that stress or the heat had overtaken him. But, he was a soldier used to extremes. I knelt by him.

"Trinity. My platoon. There was a roadside bomb."

"What are you craving, Trinity?" mom asked.

"It's the weirdest thing, I want *fritada*." In all my life, I never tried it once. "Yuck! Maybe I just want to smell it. Oh, maybe some *empanada*. Something spicy and fried."

"Where in Oceanside will I find that, huh? I'll see what I can pick up from the Mexican market after I get Tano from school."

"Try Seafood Palace, that Filipino market I took you to. Order the *dinuguan* from the buffet. I'll just smell it. It's close enough to *fritada*. You and Vance get to actually eat it."

"Show me again how to work the GPS on your phone, Trin. And, keep your feet up, they're swelling like the incredible hulk. I had to stop Tano from coloring your feet green to take a picture yesterday while you napped."

"*Ai,* mom. You should know the roads by now, it's been a month. Just use Guam style navigation. Turn at the second light, then left at the fire station."

"You're so funny. Have you and Vance decided on a name for the *neni* or what?"

"We have one for a girl, but not a boy. We really just want to be surprised when the baby arrives."

><><><

Vance rushed me to the hospital. Contractions began minutes after having a whiff of the *dinuguan*. I was overcome with missing my father, with the events of the last year. Within minutes, my water broke.

Tano took his position with his grandmother in the backseat. He bounced with excitement about the arrival of his brother or sister.

"Mommy, how are you feeling?"

"I'm okay, my son." I gasped from a contraction, but tried to sound normal.

"Do you know what today is?" Tano asked.

"Tuesday, the 19th?"

"It's the day that Tata came home from the hospital last year."

I became quiet and so did Vance and my mom. Even when the next wave of contractions hit me, I remembered the day my dad was well enough to be home in his own bed. We celebrated with some unhealthy Chamorro food. We enjoyed a little bit of karaoke—dad just swaying to each song, and then we watched a movie, all squeezed together on their bed. I felt drenched in sadness as I thought about the fact that my dad would never know this new child.

"Vance, it would do you some good to learn from our son." I said to break the silence.

"Learn what?" Vance laughed and looked at our son in the rearview mirror.

"How to remember dates."

"Mommy, everything happens for a reason." Tano was looking outside as we reached the bottom of the hill to the military hospital.

"Son? Why did you say that?" My throat went dry as I remembered my father saying this to me before he died, aside from I love you. My mom squeezed my shoulder from the back seat.

"Tata told me that."

Mom and I asked simultaneously, "When?"

"I dreamt of him last night. He was smiling. He said he missed us and he told me to take care of my baby sister."

Vance reached for my hand as the sentry waved us through. I looked down at my swollen belly, certain that my son's dream was right. It confirmed my own intuition. My tears made spots on my lavender maternity blouse.

"Mommy, so what are we naming my sister because Tata said the ocean was nice. I'm not sure what he meant."

"Tano. This is your baby sister, Genevieve Tasi Borja."

OFF ROAD

"Sometimes when someone strips you down, seemingly destroys you—you rise to become more of your actual self….from the rubble, I rise."—**Kwahu Caleb Sahmea "Tears on the Trail"**

The rapid clicking and the bright flashes from the sea of cameras echoed a time I hadn't thought about for a decade. It took me a moment to remember where I was. I looked down on the blood red carpet and my feet could not move.

"Greg?" My mom was by my side and my agent close behind. The only two people I care about in this world and the two things anchoring me to the present time.

"Hey, mom." She clutched my arm and looked up at me, smiling.

"*Kao mamaolek ha' hao?*" I knew mom spoke to me in Chamorro because she didn't want Rocco in on my stress. We looked at each other and our eyes bridged an understanding. Hearing my agent's gruff voice hauled me back to reality.

"What's the hold up peeps?" Rocco pushed us along the red carpet. "Let's keep this star parade moving. They're loving you, Tai." Mom and I exchanged glances again. Nobody in the press was shouting for me.

I was so close to Charlize Theron that I could smell her floral perfume. I glanced at her glittering gold dress and pondered if it cost more than my yearly rent. Her pitbull publicist ushered her along with a firm push on the small of her back.

In the roar, I thought I heard my name. Or maybe I was fooling myself. I was considered a newcomer even though I had been in ten films and several television dramas, my favorite being *House*. Nothing like playing a dying Yakuza gang member and having Dr. House poking, prodding and diagnosing me. Who else from Barrigada, Guam could claim that?

"Hey, Tai! Look here! You look great! Smile, please! Who's the lovely date?" I thought I was hearing things again, until my mom flicked my ear with her middle finger. It would be like my mother to do such a thing in such a public forum. I gave her a quick wide-eyed stare that said, *I cannot believe you just did that!* Maybe it was me, but it seemed that the camera flashes worked overtime then. Mom smiled and pointed in the direction of the request. I calmly looked for the source, which came from an Asian man whose booming voice didn't match his Danny DeVito stature.

I hated being called Tai by the press, but even the most literate person couldn't pronounce my Chamorro last name with the correct emphasis. I was known as Christian Tai in the business; my agent's suggestion. He didn't think my real name, Gregorio Gumataotao Taitingfong III would fly. One benefit of changing my name was breaking the chain connecting me to my dead father.

Mom released my arm as we discussed, so I could have solo shots taken. I did my usual, brooding stance with hands loose at my side, some smiles, some smolder. I hoped mom didn't leave wrinkles on the sleeve of my rented Gucci suit. I offered the ridiculous faces my acting coach made me practice in front of the mirror.

There was one constant question that streamed through my mind that night, "What the hell am I doing here?"

※ ※ ※

"Greg! What the hell are you doing here?" My father yelled. It was the night I decided to follow him. The same day I got my driver's license. My father did not go to his brother's house to turn wrenches as he told my mom. It was a motel instead.

That summer something changed in the dynamics of my parents' marriage. Mom began drinking and dad became interested in things outside the family circle. Fights in my home were never hushed, blame and insult were catapulted at everyone in the house. I did my best to shield my mom from his anger. I needed to know what caused my father to become a monster.

His red truck was parked at Motel *Maina*. I don't remember parking my mom's Camry next to the truck or even reaching the stairwell where I saw my father ascending. I looked up at the man I once worshipped, praying that he could give me a good reason he was at a motel. "What the hell are *you* doing here?" My fists clenched and the keys to my mom's car dug into my palm, but it was nothing in comparison to mom's pain.

"I'm helping someone out." My father jingled the keys with the motel's orange keychain and looked behind him nervously. "Go, home boy."

"No. I want to know where you go every week. Why mom's best friend is her beer lately. And, do you even care that I got my license today?" I took another step up.

My father's lips tightened into a straight line and he took a backwards step up, finally on the second floor. "Like I said, boy, go home. I don't owe you any explanations."

At the top of the stairs, a woman approached. She was dressed in a fitted yellow top and a short skirt. She looked a few years older than me and called out, "Greggy?" Her singsong tone told me they were more than friends.

"Who is she?" the questioned rolled out of my mouth like thunder. My father's wide eyes flashed his fear and shame.

"She's my niece. I'm helping her out with something. Now get out of here, Greg!"

"You're doing your niece?" The look on the woman's face told me my father was lying about the niece part.

"She's not a blood relative." I took another step towards my father and he stood firm on the landing. "Grace! Take the keys. Get to the room."

"What's so important that you have to meet at a filthy motel?" I punched the wall next to me--my budding dramatic flair on display.

"Son, let's go home." I took the final step up and met my father eye to eye. It was like he was seeing me for the first time. Months of him occupied with an affair and he didn't notice that I reached him in both height and girth. "Come on, let's go home to mom."

"But, your niece, Grace is waiting for your help, you dog!" My father raised his fist and cranked it back. I didn't flinch. Part of me hoped my dad's punch would force me to roll down the stairs and break my neck, but I couldn't leave my mom alone in this world. I was spared by an angry man pounding on Grace's motel door.

"Open this door! Grace!" The man was tall, strong and youthful. He banged the butt of his gun on the door frantically, then turned his attention to my father and me.

"Boy. Go home to mom." My father's hushed voice dripped with fear and he pushed me back towards the stairs.

What followed happened so quickly, I wasn't sure it was real. I heard a pop. My father's eyes went wide and he clutched onto me. I heard Grace wailing, then another pop silenced her. The man slumped over Grace as my father collapsed at my feet. The blood from his neck seeped into my sneakers, but I couldn't move. It was like I wasn't there. I was invisible.

An old man opened his door, looked from left to right and saw the blood stained concrete. Like a turtle, he retreated into his shell. The man who shot my father and his mistress sobbed. He pulled the gun up from his side and looked at me. His eyes were dark, but sad. I did not feel threatened. Somehow, I knew he had no beef with me. I remained still, then in one swift move, he placed the gun under his chin and pulled the trigger.

The plush velvet seats of the Kodak Theater were large enough for mom to be comfortable. We were near the aisle and mom couldn't contain her excitement at being seated next to Mr. Eastwood's wife. My supporting role as a disfigured Native American got me good reviews and being in an Eastwood film outweighed the fact that I was criticized for taking a role when I was in fact a Pacific Islander. Getting a nod from the Academy and finding myself at this awards show muzzled naysayers.

"This is so exciting. I am very proud of you, my boy. I told you moving to California would be the best thing that happened to you."

Mom was correct in some regard, but I felt a stab of anxiety knowing that the reason I moved here was because of my father. His death was the precipice for a new life on the mainland. Mom and I made our escape to her sister's home in Los Angeles. When Aunt Lola died, we had sunk our roots so deeply that we didn't want to return to Guam. We didn't want to face my father's family who felt that I had played a part in his demise.

I knew better, but I secretly didn't want to win tonight. I didn't want more focus on me--not from the press asking about my real name and my father, not from obscure family asking for passes to premieres and not from my grandmother who disowned me after her eldest son was murdered. I am a proud son of Guam and that's as far as the U.S. press gets; Guam press was another beast.

The awards ceremony moved along in a blur. I held on to my seat and cemented a smile on my face. When the category for best supporting actor came up, the winners from last year read our names aloud. The short clip of me on the huge screen was unbearable. I kept my eyes on my mom who watched like it was her first time. I couldn't fight a smile. I was simply happy that I could provide for her.

"You're going to get it boy." Mom whispered. Mr. Eastwood reached out to shake my hand. Rocco grabbed my shoulders from his seat behind me. The seconds that led up to the announcement was like waiting for a tsunami that was not to come. I blocked out visions of my father's face and took a deep breath.

"For his stunning portrayal of *Kwahu Caleb Sahmea,* the Oscar for best supporting actor goes to Christian Tai! Tears on the Trail!"

CHAMORRO WORD/PHRASE KEY

Agat: Village in Southern Guam, Chamorro term, Hagat

Ai: an interjection (wow/oh)

ai ádai: an expression (such as, oh my goodness)

buñelos aga': typically fried, banana doughnuts

bunita: beautiful, pretty

chagi: to try

Chamorrita: a young, Chamorro female

chenchule': a gift, usually money or food for a special occasion/death (ika)

dagan: butt

dinuguan: Filipino pork dish

Dispensa yo'. "Excuse me."

donne': red chili peppers

empanada: a meat/rice filled pastry, typically fried- with red (achiote seed colored) crust

Eskuelan Pale': Sunday school, religious instruction-eskuelan (school) / pale' (priest)

esta: indicating completion, or said when parting

este: this

fan: please

finadene': sauce consisting of soy sauce, vinegar or lemon, onions and peppers

fritada: stewed pork dish distinguished by the use of most of the pig including blood

Guahu si: "I am…"

guihan: fish

guma: home/house

ha'ani: day

Hafa Adai: common Chamorro greeting, "Hello."

Hafa tatamanu hao? "How are you?"

hayi: who?

hunggan: yes

ika: donation for relatives of the deceased (**chenchule'** commonly substituted)

kaduka: indicating a "crazy" female

Kao mamaolek ha'hao? "How are you doing?"

kelaguen: food dish defined by the addition of lemon juice, including onions, peppers and shredded coconut/typically made with barbecue chicken, shrimp or fish

laña: an expletive phrase which was once taboo/ used to express surprise, anger or disgust

latiya: Chamorro dessert, yellow cake topped with custard and cinnamon

latte stone: stone pillar (haligi and tasa), symbol used as a symbol of Chamorro identity, used as base of ancient homes

maila halom: come in

Malesso': village of Merizo, southern Guam

mamalao: shy, ashamed

mangge: where?

manu: where

muyo': expression of disgust or anger, disapproving face

nana: mother

neni: baby, infant/term of endearment

palao'an: female, girl

Pale': priest

pika: spicy

Sa hafa? Why/what?

Si Yu'os Ma'ase: literally-"God Have Mercy." Used to express thanks.

sigi magi: come here

Siñora: female teacher

Siñot: male teacher

Sirena: mythical mermaid character of Guam legend

siya: chair, seat

susu: breasts

Tan: used as term of respect for older female, madame

Taotao Hagåtña yo'. "I am from Agana."

tasi: ocean

tata: father

tataga': unicorn fish

techa: one who leads a rosary, prayer

titiyas: tortillas (corn/flour)

Todu maolek. "All is good."

Tomhom: Village in northern Guam, known as Tumon

yan: and

Yigo: Village in northern Guam

zori *(yore'): slippers, "flip flops", Japanese sandal

About the Author

Tanya Chargualaf Taimanglo was born in 1974 to a Chamorro Army soldier and a South Korean beauty, Un Cha Kang. Her father is the late Siñot Tedy Gamboa Chargualaf. Tanya is the eldest child of three. Her mom and brothers, Theo and Sonny K. Chargualaf reside on Guam with their families. Sonny created the cover and title art for this book in addition to their children's book, *Sirena: A Mermaid Legend from Guam*.

Tanya is the product of a Guam public school education. She graduated in 1992 from George Washington High School. She attended the University of Guam on a Merit Scholarship. She graduated with honors with a BA in English and Secondary Education in 1996. Tanya had an eight year career as an English and Creative Writing teacher at John F. Kennedy High School; working proudly with the Tourism Academy. She taught alongside her late father, a Chamorro teacher and brother, Sonny--an art teacher. She has had work featured in Latte Magazine (*Chirika's Pepper Plant*), University of Guam's Storyboard 6 and articles in local business magazines. She received the Who's Who Among America's Teachers award in 2000 and 2002. Her short story, *Yes, I Am.*, will be included in an anthology featuring Pacific Islander writers in 2011, *USO's on Freeways*.

Tanya married her childhood friend, Henry Taimanglo--a Navy Chief, in 2004 in the village of Asan, Guam. They currently reside in California with their two children. Tanya volunteers with the non-profit organization, CHE'LU, Inc. which strives to promote the Chamorro culture through education.

Breinigsville, PA USA
28 September 2010
246201BV00001B/21/P